T0343916

EDITOR'S LETTER

A climate of fear

Editor **MARTIN BRIGHT** says environmental campaigners and indigenous peoples in particular must not be silenced

THE FIGHT FOR the future of the planet and the fight for free speech are intertwined and interdependent. But, like any healthy ecological system, this relationship also needs constant nurturing. This is the aim of the Autumn issue of Index on Censorship, themed around the struggle for environmental justice with a particular focus on indigenous campaigners. In advance of the United Nations climate change conference (COP26), held in Glasgow in November, we have decided to concentrate the cases of people whose voices are too easily forgotten in this debate. Emily Brown interviews Yvonne Weldon, the first aboriginal candidate for Mayor of Sydney, who is fighting on an environmental platform.

Meanwhile, Kaya Genç examines the conspiracy theories and threats swirling around green campaigners in Turkey. Issa Sikiti da Silva exposes the openly hostile conditions faced by environmental activists in Uganda and Beth Pitts talks

to two indigenous activists in Ecuador on declining populations and how they are using modern campaigning methods to save their culture and fight the extraction companies.

The issue also contains an exclusive piece on press freedom by Mikhail Khodorkovsky, the Russian businessman jailed for nine years when he fell foul of the Putin regime and an interview with a second Putin opponent, the US financier Bill Browder by celebrated British journalist John Sweeney.

A critical role of this publication is to remind the world of conflicts and regime abuses that have faded from international attention. As courageous demonstrators continue to take to the streets in Belarus, the regime is systematically closing down organised opposition in the country, including all but the most loyal media organisations. This is why we are proud to publish letters from Lukashenka's prisoners to remind people of the brave struggle for democracy.

Index went to press as Kabul fell

to the Taliban. It is therefore right that we pay tribute to the artists and writers in Afghanistan who have built a flourishing cultural legacy over the past two decades. We are proud to publish two poems by the award-winning British Afghan writer Parwana Fayyaz from her recent collection Forty Names. These include Her Name is Flower Sap, a remarkable poem about Sharbet Gula, the green-eyed girl who stared out from a 1995 edition of National Geographic magazine and became a symbol for her country's suffering. This extract stands as an epigraph to this edition of Index:

'Her eyes have the magic of good and bad.'
'The light of her eyes can destroy fighter jets.'

So went Afghan children's conversation in the aftermath of 9/11. 'But could she take down

The Taliban jets,' we wondered, as the jets crossed the skies in one song.

But Flower Sap could never answer us. For she had disappeared like our childhood. ✖

Martin Bright is editor of *Index on Censorship*

50(03):01/01|DOI:10.1177/03064220211048850

A delicate balance

MARK FRARY introduces our cover artist **WILSON BORJA**

Wilson Borja (**wilsonborja.com**) was born and raised in Bogotá. He studied graphic design and has worked in illustration and animation.

His recent work has been inspired by the African diaspora

and migration and his last exhibition pre-Covid at Bogotà's African Diaspora Gallery in 2019 was focused on this topic.

Borja likes to mix digital and physical elements in his work. This issue's illustration includes

plant species Borja collected from the Pacific coast of Colombia, where most of the population is of African descent.

LEFT: Wilson Borja

CONTENTS

Culture

....

The Index

A round-up of events in the world of free expression from Index's unparalleled network of writers and activists. Edited by **MARK FRARY**

PICTURED: Graffiti artist Shamsia Hassani, born in 1988, is the first female graffiti artist of Afghanistan. Her work portrays Afghan women in a male-dominated society and has inspired thousands of women around the world and gave a new hope to female Afghan artists in the country. Her future under the Taliban remains unclear.

The Index

THE GREAT SCEPTIC

MY INSPIRATION

Cambridge philosopher **ARIF AHMED** writes about his eminent predecessor Bertrand Russell

THE GREAT CAMBRIDGE philosopher Bertrand Russell was born in 1872. His first interest was logic – the most secure of all sciences, he thought. His obsessional (if doomed) quest to base mathematics upon logic led to the monumental Principia Mathematica of 1912.

During WW1 he supported conscientious objectors and campaigned doggedly for pacifism. In the 1920s he advocated free love and ran an experimental school. From the 1950s he protested against nuclear weapons and helped start CND. On his deathbed he still fought, for the Palestinian people.

He persisted through censorship and imprisonment. In 1916 he lost his job at Cambridge because of his pacifism. In 1918 he spent six months in prison for opposing American involvement in the war. In 1941 he was fired from the College of the city of New York, because his works were deemed 'erotomaniac... narrow-minded, untruthful and bereft of moral fibre'.

But what really drove Russell was not (or not only) sex but scepticism: scepticism of authority and of conventional wisdom. Philosophical truth comes from thinking for yourself – using logic and experience – not from 'common sense' or dogma. Political freedom means choosing for yourself, not following the plans of a supposedly benevolent central power.

This independence surfaced in his attitude to post-revolutionary Russia, which he visited when Western intellectuals were falling over themselves to idolise the communist regime. Russell saw right through it. As he later wrote: 'The dangers of irresponsible power came to be generally recognised during the 18th and 19th centuries, but those who have been dazzled by the outward success of the Soviet Union have forgotten all that was painfully learned during the days of absolute monarchy, and have gone back to what was worst in the Middle Ages under the curious delusion that they were in the vanguard of progress.'

Bertrand Russell was the leading defender of Enlightenment values – rational thought, scepticism, individual liberty – in a century that increasingly found them naïve. They are not naïve; they are precious. As we learn from Russell's example, the freedom of the individual to think and speak for herself is our best defence against the soft totalitarianism now threatening Britain and the rest of the nominally free world. ✖

Arif Ahmed is a philosopher

ABOVE: Bertrand Russell pictured in 1962 during the Cuban Missile Crisis

Free speech in numbers

11

Sentence in years given to Belarusian opposition activist Maria Kalesnikova in September

50,000

The number of phones infected with Pegasus spyware revealed on a list leaked in July

10

The number of days it took the Afghan government to collapse after the departure of US troops

227

people died defending their homes, land and livelihoods, and ecosystems vital for biodiversity and the climate during 2020.
Source: Global Witness

26

The number of years that Apple Daily provided news to the people of Hong Kong before it was forced to close under the National Security Law

YOU MAY HAVE MISSED

BENJAMIN LYNCH rounds up important news on free expression from around the world

First sentencing under HK's National Security Law

Tong Ying-kit became the first person to be sentenced to jail under China's oppressive National Security Law.

The 24-year-old was sentenced to nine years imprisonment after being found guilty of terrorism and inciting secession. This came after he drove a motorbike into a group of police officers while carrying a flag that read "Liberate Hong Kong, revolution of our times".

The law has been used to target journalists and activists across China and Hong Kong very severely

US student wins free speech case

A high school cheerleader won an important victory for the right of students to express their opinions freely while off campus.

At the end of June, the US Supreme Court - which was asked to consider whether schools had the right to regulate off-campus speech – ruled eight to one that the rights of high school student Brandi Levy had been violated in 2017.

After failing to make the varsity cheerleading team, Levy had posted profanity-laced criticisms of the team roster on Snapchat while off campus at a local convenience store.

Jonathan Taylor extradition request dropped

The case against whistleblower Jonathan Taylor was finally dropped after the Croatian justice minister rejected the request by Monaco to extradite him.

The former lawyer worked for Monaco-based SBM Offshore and blew the whistle on a major bribery scandal.

Legal to Say. Legal to Type

Index, along with David Davis MP and Gavin Millar QC have criticised the UK government's online safety bill.

The bill in its current form would be damaging to free speech, in that it would set into stone a difference in the law that makes certain speech illegal online, but legal in the street. Fines for social media firms not taking down content would likely see over-cautiousness from them, meaning any social media post would under much stricter control.

Index launched the "Legal to Say. Legal to Type" campaign in June, to scrutinise the bill. ✖

The ink assassin

THE WORK OF award-winning Ecuadorian cartoonist Xavier Bonilla, better known as Bonil, has appeared in most of the country's major publications including national newspaper El Universo and magazines such as Nuestro Mundo.

He has frequently been targeted for his caricatures of Ecuador's leaders. In 2013, a cartoon satirising an illegal police raid led former president Rafale Correa to call Bonil an "ink assassin". He has been dragged to court many times and has been fined by Ecuador's Superintendent of Information and Communication for his work.

Last year, Bonil received threats on social media from Bucaram Pulley, the son of former President Abdalá Bucaram Ortiz, after Bonil drew a cartoon that depicted Pulley fleeing authorities. Pulley had disappeared after a judge issued a warrant for his arrest for his alleged involvement in the sale of overpriced medical supplies to public hospitals dealing with the Covid-19 pandemic.

Recently his work has covered the fall of Afghanistan to the Taliban, the Ecuadorean judiciary, Covid and the environment. ✖

This cartoon, entitled Plastic, was published in 2019

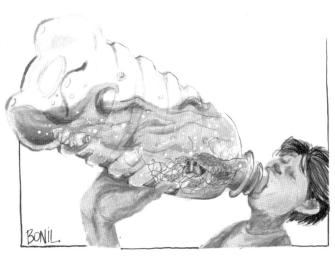

The Index

PEOPLE WATCH

BENJAMIN LYNCH highlights the stories of a Bahraini academic and targeted journalists in Belarus and Morocco

Dr Abdujalil al-Singace

ACTIVIST AND ENGINEER - BAHRAIN

Various rights groups – including PEN International – were joint signatories in the latest calls to release imprisoned Bahraini academic Dr Abdulljalil al-Singace.

The opposition activist is serving a life sentence after being arrested during the pro-democracy movements in 2011.

Since 8 July, he has been on a hunger strike protesting the conditions of Jau Prison, where he is being held. Reports have previously alleged that Alsingace has been subjected to repeated torture and sexual assault.

Siarhei Hardziyevich

JOURNALIST - BELARUS

In August, Hardziyevich, a 50-year-old journalist from Drahichyn, a city 300km south-west of Minsk, was sentenced to one and a half years in prison for slander of the Belarusian authorities and insulting President Lukashenko.

Hardziyevich was a journalist at the 1reg.by website and news outlet The First Region.

The messages were on a now deleted group chat on messaging app Viber but the journalist has protested his innocence and has been dubbed a political prisoner by human rights centre Viasna.

Vitaly Shishov

ACTIVIST - BELARUS

Vitaly Shishov from Belarus went missing while in the neighbouring country of Ukraine after leaving home to go jogging. His body was later found hanged in a Kiev park.

Shishov was a high-profile dissident and head of the Belarusian House in Ukraine (BDU), which helps people fleeing the country. Friends of the activist have said that before Shishov was found dead, he was followed by "strangers".

Ukrainian police have since opened an investigation into his possible murder.

Omar Radi

JOURNALIST - MOROCCO

A critic of the Moroccan government, Omar Radi was sentenced to six years in prison on 19 July.

He was accused of espionage and rape, but his treatment during the trial has been questioned.

According to Amnesty International, Radi's legal team "were denied the right to access some of the evidence against him and all requests to summon defence witnesses".

It has also been reported that Radi's mobile phone was targeted by the Pegasus spyware. ✖

Reporting human rights violations in Turkey

VEYSEL OK, free speech lawyer and co-director of the Media and Law Studies Association (MLSA), says journalists who contradict the State are increasingly put on trial

On 13 September 2020, Cemil Uğur from Mesopotamia News Agency (MA) reported about two Kurdish villagers who were abducted and tortured by security forces in Van's Çatak district during military operations against the Kurdistan Workers' Party (PKK). On 6 October, the office of MA was raided and

Uğur was detained together with his colleague Adnan Bilen from MA, reporter Şehriban Abi and freelance journalist Nazan Sala.

All the detained journalists had reported on the torture of the two villagers and were arrested on 9 October on the grounds of "reporting on social incidents against

the state" and were charged with "being members of an armed organisation". The four defendants, of whom MLSA represents Uğur, Abi and Sala, were released in the first hearing of the trial on 2 April under judicial control measures. MLSA continues to offer support.

In Turkey, human rights are being continuously and

increasingly violated by the state. Journalists who report these violations are among those who are prosecuted the most. Deeply committed to freedom of speech and freedom of expression, MLSA **mlsaturkey.com** has always been and will continue to be on the side of journalists who are prosecuted simply for doing their jobs to inform the public. ✖

CHAMPIONS OF FREE EXPRESSION CELEBRATED IN AWARDS

The winners of Index on Censorship's 2021 Freedom of Expression awards were announced at a ceremony in London on 12 September hosted by actor and writer Tracy-Ann Oberman

THE FREEDOM OF Expression Awards, which were first held in 2000, celebrate individuals or groups who have had a significant impact fighting censorship anywhere in the world. Winners join Index's Awards Fellowship programme and receive dedicated training and support. This year's awards are particularly significant, coming as the organisation celebrates its 50th birthday.

Winners were announced in three categories - art, campaigning and journalism - and a fourth Trustees Award was also presented.

The 2021 Trustees Award was presented to **Arif Ahmed**. Ahmed is a free speech activist and fellow of Gonville & Caius College at the University of Cambridge. In March 2020, Ahmed proposed alterations to the Statement of Free Speech at Cambridge. The proposed amendments were created to make the legislation "clearer and more liberal." He aimed to protect university campuses as places of innovation and invention.

The 2021 Freedom of Expression Award for Journalism was presented to **Samira Sabou**. Sabou is a Nigerien journalist, blogger and president of the Niger Bloggers for Active Citizenship Association (ABCA). In June 2020, Sabou was arrested and charged with defamation under the restrictive 2019 cybercrime law in connection with a comment on her Facebook post highlighting corruption. Sabou is also active in promoting girls' and women's right to freedom of expression.

The 2021 Freedom of Expression Award for Art was presented to **Tatyana Zelenskaya**. Zelenskaya is an illustrator from Kyrgyzstan, working on freedom of expression and women's rights projects. Zelenskaya has found inspiration for her work in the waves of anti-government protests that have recently erupted across Russia and Kyrgyzstan. In 2020, she created the artwork for a narrative video game called Swallows: Spring in Bishkek, which features a woman who helps her friend that was abducted and forced into an unwanted marriage. The game was downloaded more than 70,000 times in its first month.

The 2021 Freedom of Expression Award for Campaigning was presented to **Abdelrahman "Moka" Tarek**. Tarek is a human rights defender from Egypt, who focuses on defending the right to freedom of expression and the rights of prisoners. Tarek has experienced frequent harassment from Egyptian authorities as a result of his work. He has spent longer periods of time in prison and has experienced torture, solitary confinement, and sexual abuse. Authorities have severely restricted his ability to communicate with his lawyer and family. Tarek was arrested again in September 2020 and in December 2020, a new case was brought against him on terrorism-related charges. Tarek began a hunger strike in protest of the terrorism charges.

ABOVE: Host Tracy-Ann Oberman speaks passionately about freedom of expression

Index on Censorship chief executive Ruth Smeeth said: "As Index marks its 50th birthday it's clear that the battle to guarantee free expression and free expression around the globe has never been more relevant. Inspired by the tremendous courage of our award winners, we will continue in our mission to defend free speech and free expression around the globe, give voice to the persecuted, and stand against repression wherever we find it".

Trevor Philips, chair of Index on Censorship, said: "Across the globe, the past year has demonstrated the power of free expression. For many the only defence is the word or image that tells the story of their repression; and for the oppressors the sound they fear most is diversity of thought and opinion. Index exists to ensure that in that battle, freedom wins - both abroad, and as this year's Trustee award demonstrates here at home too." ✖

50(04):04/11|DOI:10.1177/03064220211048851

The Index

World In Focus: Cuba

Alexander Lukashenko's crackdown on peaceful protest and the media has continued, the most notable of which was the forced grounding of a plane carrying journalist and activist Roman Protasevich. But incidents have happened elsewhere in the country too.

1 Camagüey

Niefe Rigau, Henry Constantin and Iris Mariño were working for independent news outlet La Hora de Ciba on 11 July when they were arrested in the province of Camagüey in central Cuba.

According to the news site, the three journalists were taken to the Technical Investigative Unit of the Ministry of the Interior, apparently known as "the place where everyone sings" due to alleged severe methods of interrogation.

The three are now detained under house arrest.

2 Havana

YouTuber, activist and independent journalist Dina Stars was arrested during a live interview with CNN on 14 July. Stars was arrested on suspicion of "promoting protests" after being critical of current Cuban president Miguel Díaz-Canel.

During the interview, Stars said: "The state's security forces are here. I have to go."

She was released on the same day and released a statement on social media that read: ""They arrested me for instigation to commit a crime, for promoting the protests. They didn't torture me. I am on the side of truth."

3 Cárdenas

The CubaNet journalist Orelvis Cabrera was arrested on 11 July while covering protests in Cárdenas, in the province of Matanzas.

Now moved to house arrest until his trial, Cabrera is charged with "public disturbances", after spending 37 days in jail before being released on 17 August.

The charge carries a minimum three-month sentence but could see him jailed for up to one year.

Defiant, he told CubaNet on his release: "I was practically buried, the cell was below ground level. It has been difficult, but I have come out with more strength. ✖

Tech watch: Pegasus

MARK FRARY on the innovations threatening freedom of expression around the world

IMAGINE THE OUTCRY if your every move, every detail of your private life, everything you uttered and everyone you met was being tracked.

Yet this is essentially what your smartphone does. Manufacturers insist there are safeguards in place to ensure this does not end up in the wrong hands.

Yet, as 50,000 activists, journalists and politicians discovered this summer, that may have already happened.

In July, the Pegasus Project, a collaboration of more than 80 journalists from 17 media organisations coordinated by Paris-based media non-profit Forbidden Stories with the technical support of Amnesty International revealed that their phones had potentially been infected by a piece of spyware called Pegasus, built by the NSO Group.

Those targeted can upload the spyware to their devices by clicking a so-called spear-phishing link or, increasingly, without their knowledge through holes in the phone's operating system. Once installed, it can copy messages and photos, record calls and secretly film the phone's owner among many other worrying things.

The revelations of the Project,

JOURNALISM UNDER ATTACK

MARK FRARY takes a look at stories that have generated the most interest on our Twitter channel. Follow us @IndexCensorship

THIS YEAR, AND just like Index on Censorship, WikiLeaks founder Julian Assange celebrated his 50th birthday. Neither is a particularly good thing to celebrate. Since 1971, Index has had to fight to be the voice of the persecuted, from Soviet dissidents to censored artists. It's work remains vital today.

As for Julian Assange, his 50th on 3 July 2021, was spent in Belmarsh prison, still awaiting an outcome of the US Government's request to extradite him over for alleged hacking and classified information disclosures, including revealing the identities of informants in Afghanistan and Iraq.

In August, Assange got an unwanted belated birthday present. Judge Baraitser has now expanded the grounds on which the US Government can appeal. The case

will be heard in late October.

The case continues to focus on whether Assange's actions are those of a journalist and should therefore be protected. Index believes they should.

Our ongoing coverage of the rapidly escalating attacks on journalists in Belarus was also widely read and shared.

Journalist Hanna Yahorava wrote (**tinyurl.com/Index503BAJ**) about the clampdown on independent journalists and the Belarusian Association of Journalists.

In July 2021, the government of Alexander Lukashenko launched a new wave of repression against independent media outlets and organisations. Over ten days, security forces carried out more than 70 searches of editorial offices and private homes of employees of national and regional media.

Now BAJ itself is in Lukashenko's sights.

The offices have been sealed and the country's Supreme Court has issued an order for the organisation to be liquidated, a fate suffered by 50 other public organisations which have been of benefit for decades to Belarusian society, journalism, the writing community and many other areas.

BAJ's closure – if the courts agree

ABOVE: Julian Assange's partner Stella Moris (centre) talks to the media outside the High Court in London at a hearing in August

to the liquidation – will cause serious damage to the Belarusian journalistic community.

"Firstly, there will be no legal organisation left in the country that can protect the rights of journalists.

Secondly, the association's educational hub for journalists will disappear, and many BAJ educational programmes will have to be closed.

Finally, the only legal and recognised institution of journalistic ethical self-government will be destroyed – the BAJ Ethics Commission. In recent years, this was the only body in Belarus that effectively considered issues related to ethics in the media," said Yahorava. ✖

in publications such as The Guardian, Le Monde and the Washington Post, showed the breathtaking reach of Pegasus.

At the core of the Project was a leaked list of 50,000 people, including journalists, activists and politicians from Azerbaijan to India, Mexico to Saudi Arabia, who had been allegedly been selected

as targets for Pegasus.

On the list were French president Emmanuel Macron, the family of murdered Saudi dissident Jamal Khashoggi, women's rights activist Loujain al-Hathloul and Mexican journalist Cecilio Pineda.

NSO Group issued a statement following the breaking of the story saying what it found was "not a list

of targets or potential targets of Pegasus" and that the claims are "erroneous and false".

The company added: "We do not operate the system, nor do we have access to the data of our customers, yet they are obligated to provide us with such information under investigations.

"NSO will continue its

mission of saving lives, helping governments around the world prevent terror attacks, break up paedophilia, sex, and drug-trafficking rings, locate missing and kidnapped children, locate survivors trapped under collapsed buildings, and protect airspace against disruptive penetration by dangerous drones." ✖

Maya Forstater: Pile-ons and censorship

A response to Phoenix Andrews' article in the summer issue of Index on Censorship

N INDEX'S SUMMER magazine Phoenix Andrews accuses me of engaging in hate speech by tweeting "about trans women being men", suggesting this should come within the ambit of the criminal offence of "threatening behaviour". This is the use of abusive words to make someone believe that they are about to be attacked, which can carry up to six months' imprisonment. It's not just shouting "fire" in a crowded theatre, it is shouting "I am going to set fire to your theatre".

It is a shocking thing to read about yourself. And obviously, no I have not threatened anybody.

What I did was express opposition, in tweets and a blogpost to the idea of the government allowing people to change sex via "gender self-identification". I made statements such as:

"What I am so surprised at is that smart people who I admire, who are absolutely pro-science in other areas, and champion human rights and women's rights are tying themselves in knots to avoid saying the truth that men cannot change into women (because that

> ## Since I won my case hundreds of people have contacted me to tell me they now feel braver.

might hurt men's feelings)."

For this I lost my job at an international development think-tank.

The first judge who heard my discrimination case thought that was as it should be; my beliefs he said are "not worthy of respect in a democratic society".

In their article in Index on Censorship, Andrews agrees.

It is an extraordinarily authoritarian view to hold.

But it is increasingly ordinary in the HR departments and Equality and Diversity units of major corporations, charities, public sector bodies and universities. Many are members of the Stonewall Diversity Champion Scheme in which they pledge allegiance to the idea of gender identity. They reward and punish staff and influence public policy, public debate and law enforcement.

So the idea that a police officer might turn up at my door at the behest of a trans rights activist, for saying that I do not believe a person with a penis is a woman, is not so far-fetched.

The police turned up at Harry Miller's workplace to "check his thinking". Miranda Yardley, a transsexual, was prosecuted for a transgender hate crime after a complainant, who worked for the charity Mermaids which promotes transitioning children alleged harassment for tweeting information already in the public domain. Kellie-Jay Keen was reported to police after she referred to Mermaids' CEO Susie Green taking her son to Thailand at the age of 16 to be castrated and have his penis fashioned into a simulation of a vagina. Linda Bellos OBE was prosecuted for

using threatening language, for saying she would use self-defence if faced by attacks by trans rights activists. Kate Scottow was prosecuted after unkindly tweeting that a particular trans identifying man was a "pig in a wig". She was arrested and held in a cell for seven hours, her computer and phone were impounded for months.

They all fought back and won. The CPS dropped the case against Linda Bellos, but not before the 70-year-old had to attend court three times. Kate Scottow's conviction for "causing annoyance, inconvenience and anxiety" was eventually overturned almost two years after her arrest. Harry Miller took Humberside Police to court and won.

Most people do not end up in court but feel this chilling effect via their workplace or profession.

Do they dare resist pressure to announce their pronouns? Can they say they don't think men should be in women's prisons or sports? What if their job involves safeguarding children, will they pretend that words can change a person's sex?

Since I launched my case hundreds of people have contacted me to say they are terrified at work, or have been bullied and harassed for being gender critical. They tell of having to defend their social media posts, facing complaints for signing letters to newspapers about academic freedom, or for saying that JK Rowling is not transphobic. They have been no platformed, blackballed and sidelined. Journalists have pronouns changed after they submit their copy, researchers find projects rejected on

People I admire, who are pro-science, are tying themselves in knots to avoid saying the truth

ABOVE: Maya Forstater won her appeal at the Employment Appeal Tribunal after losing her job for saying people cannot change their biological sex

vague suspicions of transphobia. Those in the public domain such as the columnist Suzanne Moore, the academics Kathleen Stock, Selina Todd and Jo Phoenix and the artists Rachel Ara and Jess de Wahl are just the tip of the iceberg.

Since I won my case hundreds of people have contacted me to tell me they now feel braver.

Others such as the barrister Allison Bailey, the Girl Guide leader Katie Alcock and the therapist James Esses are taking discrimination cases to court.

If anyone considers my words constitute criminal activity, they should be aware that Justice Julian Knowles said of the complainant who reported Harry Miller's tweets her outrage was "at times, at the outer margins of rationality."

To make matters worse, my views on the response to the Andrews article are now being censored.

After the Lesbian, Gay and Bisexual Alliance tweeted a criticism of the article, Andrews reported being under attack and facing a "pile-on". Almost a hundred academics, journalists and others responded with tweeted messages of solidarity for Andrews.

I did not consider that a pile-on was happening and I documented this in a blog post which I published on Medium.

My blog posts featured "receipts": screenshots of the public tweets and responses, and links to Twitter searches showing that there was no "pile-on".

Then I received an email from Medium saying my post (and another in relation to

a separate issue) were under investigation.

I was asked to "remove all personally identifying information". Of course I didn't. How could I respond to Andrews' article without naming them?

A little later I received a second email. The investigation was complete. My posts were removed.

"Site policies prohibit posts that name specific private individuals for the purpose of targeted harassment or shaming, especially where doing so is likely to incite or foster further harassment, threats, and violence."

I am now left arguing with the algorithmic censors that I did not name Andrews to harass or shame them, nor to incite "further harassment, threats and violence", but in order to make sense of my response to their claims about me and the response to my article. ✖

50(03):12/13|DOI:10.1177/03064220211048852

'Deeply serious and transformational poetry'

JENNY LEWIS

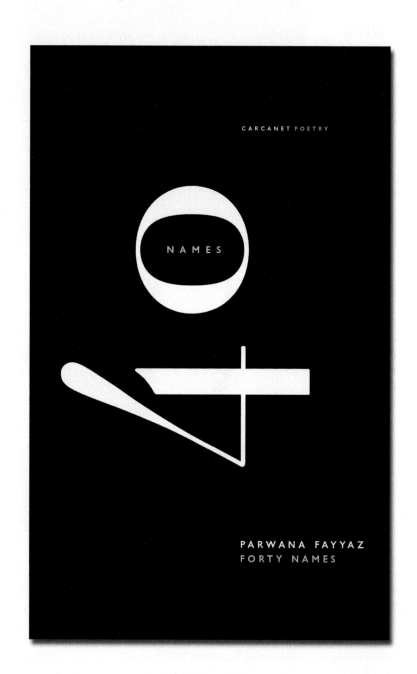

FORTY NAMES

PARWANA FAYYAZ

£10.99 / 978 1 80017 107 7 / CARCANET POETRY

CARCANET

FEATURES

"I used to think I was the person the Kremlin hated
the most, certainly the top foreigner they hated"

BILL BROWDER ON FALLING OUT WITH THE WRONG PEOPLE IN RUSSIA | THE WEST IS FRIGHTENED OF CONFRONTING THE BULLY P16

The West is frightened of confronting the bully

BILL BROWDER tells **JOHN SWEENEY** about his guilt over the death of Sergei Magnitsky and what makes Vladimir Putin tick

THE SECOND MOST interesting fact about William Felix "Bill" Browder is that his grandfather, Earl Browder, was the general secretary of the Communist Party of the USA, and Bill became an uber-capitalist to piss off his folks.

He started off buying Russia's $1 billion Arctic fishing fleet for a fiver – I'm not sure those numbers are exact, but you get the gist.

Browder, ever the ornery bastard, then became a tough investor in Russian business, asking questions, raising hell about corrupt payments, standing up for shareholders' rights.

For a time, in 1997, his company, Hermitage Capital, was the best-performing fund in the world. Then the weather changed in Russia and he fell out with the wrong kind of people.

The most interesting fact about Bill Browder is that he is the foreigner most hated by the master of the Kremlin, Vladimir Putin. Russia's strongman president has had a great 2021. The West is in retreat after the defeat in Kabul, his only political rival, Alexei Navalny is safely behind bars, the activist's anti-corruption network rolled up, and Kremlin-friendly oligarchs are strutting through London's law courts as if they own them, allegedly. But Browder's tank remains on the Kremlin's lawn. Russia has tried eight times to have Browder extradited, in vain.

Unable to snuff him out, the Russian secret state killed his tax lawyer, Sergei Magnitsky. Browder went to war and, so far, more than 30 countries – starting with the USA – have passed Magnitsky Acts aimed at targeting corrupt officials from Russia and elsewhere.

Over a Zoom call, Browder goes through what the Russian state did to put pressure on Magnitsky to climb down after he had discovered a complex fraud by senior tax officials – a fraud that started with redirecting Hermitage's

------

MAIN: Vladimir Putin at the Kremlin, 2007

tax payments of some $230 million.

"They put him in all sorts of terrible situations. They kept the lights on 24 hours a day to impose sleep deprivation. They put him in cells with no heat and no window panes in December, in Moscow. They moved him from cell to cell to cell," he says.

"And the purpose of all this was to get him to withdraw his testimony against the corrupt officers. He refused. The torture got worse and worse, he ended up getting sick. He ended up losing 20kg, developing terrible pains in his stomach.

"He was diagnosed as having pancreatitis and gall stones. They refused him any medical treatment. He and his lawyers wrote 20 different desperate requests for medical treatment to every branch of the criminal justice system.

"All those requests were ignored or denied. And on the night of 16 November 2009, almost 12 years ago, he went into a critical condition. The authorities, instead of putting him in an emergency room, put him in an isolation cell. They chained him to a bed, and riot guards with rubber truncheons beat him until he died.

"At the age of 37, he left a wife and two children. And when I got that news, it was the most traumatic, life-changing, horrific news I could have ever gotten. And I made a vow to his memory, to his family and myself that I was going to put aside everything else that I was doing, and devote all of my time all of my resources and all of my energies to go after the people who killed him and make sure they face justice.

"And for the last almost 12 years, that's what I've been doing."

I put it to Browder that the Kremlin couldn't kill him so they got Magnitsky instead. Does he feel some measure of guilt about that?

"Completely. I feel guilty every day about that, I feel it. And that's the driving force of my life, the guilt.

"If he hadn't been my lawyer, he'd still be alive today. And that plagues me.

Deep down, the British government and many other governments are scared of Putin

And that's a burden on my shoulders that I'll never be able to free myself from."

Time was when Browder was the Kremlin's number-one target.

"I used to think I was the person that they hated the most – certainly the foreigner they hated the most," he says.

"But that's been replaced for sure by Alexei Navalny. Most people are too scared to stand up to them and, as a result, they end up getting away with a lot of stuff. But I stood up to them after what happened with Sergei Magnitsky. And we drew blood in the form of all these sanctions, which is something that they never expected.

"So they really, desperately, wanted to make an example out of me in order to prevent anyone else from seeing that they aren't as all-powerful as they make themselves out to be."

It's a lonely business, drawing blood from the Kremlin. Navalny and Browder have succeeded. Most Western politicians suffer from eternal optimism, misreading Putin, the gangster-trained, psychopathically-vengeful former KGB officer as a Mr Barrowclough, the pitifully nice warder from British sitcom Porridge, but with snow on his boots.

I ask Browder to explain why he thought the West kept on being fooled by Mr Barrowcloughski or, rather, Vlad the Poisoner.

"The most dramatic and stark example is the case of the 2018 Salisbury poisonings in the UK," he says.

"Here, actors from the Russian state, dispatched by Vladimir Putin, came ➜

→ to the UK with a military grade nerve agent and administered it to one of their enemies, Sergei Skripal, creating a massive public health emergency in a British city. They closed the whole city down and we ended up having the death of an innocent bystander, Dawn Sturgess.

"You have a police officer whose life was ruined by this whole thing. And what was the consequence of that? They expelled a bunch of diplomats.

"And the unspoken secret about expelling diplomats is that they then replace them with other diplomats. And so there was no consequence. And why was there no consequence? Because, deep down, the British government and many other governments are scared of Putin.

"They don't want to actually pick a fight with him. They're scared. And so they want to seem to be doing the right thing but they don't actually want to do the right thing.

"And so we ended up in a world where Putin gets away with murder, literally, on a regular basis around the world.

"Look at what's happened with the United States. The Russians were paying the Taliban to kill American soldiers. Has anything happened? No. They were hacking pipelines. Has anything happened? No. We've given Putin a pass for far too long."

Browder fears that part of the problem of gauging Putin accurately is democracy itself. Each new Western leader feels they can get a grip on the little man in the Kremlin.

He says: "Every time we get a new leader coming in, they look at the terrible relationship that Britain and the United States has with Russia, and the new leader comes in very arrogantly and self-confidently, saying, 'Well, you know, my predecessor really didn't know how to deal with this, but I know how to deal with him and I'm going to charm him or I'm going to reset relations and make things right'. And time and again Putin ends up laughing at them.

"It just carries on and on. Nobody wants to put their foot down and say enough is enough. We need to contain Russia – no more of this pussyfooting around. Nobody yet has the guts to really stand up to him among the leaders in the West."

I ask him what he would do.

"Well, it's real simple. And it doesn't require a huge amount of risk-taking.

"Putin is not going to go to war with us, because he would lose. He has a very sclerotic military – the military budget of Russia is the same as the UK's.

"Russia's economy is tiny, so he doesn't really have any normal, confrontational tools to fight us.

"What he does is all this asymmetric fighting, hacking elections, doing all this kind of stuff. But we also have some asymmetric tools.

"The main weakness of Vladimir Putin, the way I see it, is that so much money has been shifted from the Russian state to his proxies that he's a thief, no a kleptocrat. He's stolen an enormous amount of money from the Russian people. He doesn't keep much of that money in Russia. He keeps the money in the West – not in his own name but in the name of oligarchs. And so how do we get what he covets the most, which

> The main weakness of Vladimir Putin, the way I see it, is that so much money has been shifted from the Russian state to his proxies that he's a thief, no a kleptocrat.

is his money? We freeze the assets of the oligarchs who look after his money.

"It's well known who those oligarchs are. Alexei Navalny published a list of these people. It's well known to all the experts and intelligence services.

"And so if we really want to stop Putin from doing all this stuff, you just freeze [their] assets, and that will get him to stop doing all the nastiness. Because what he cares about more than anything is his money."

Does Browder know why it hasn't happened?

"It's fear of confronting a bully. Nobody wants to take that on."

In the meantime, the ratchet of fear in Russia is being tightened. Some of it is just plain mad, such as the prosecution of Magnitsky after his death. The corpse was found guilty.

Some of it is common murder. And it is getting closer to home. The chilling effect of Roman Abramovich's libel action against Catherine Belton for her book, Putin's People, has been felt in London.

Journalists who write on Russia are running scared. If they aren't, their editors and their lawyers are – and with good reason.

The rights and wrongs of the case are yet to be heard but what is the general effect? Well, it smacks of a new, post-modern kind of censorship. Shut your mouth or you will lose a lot of money.

One of my favourite books is A Cup of Coffee with My Interrogator, by the Czech dissident Ludvik Vaculik, translated by Index stalwart George Theiner. Vaculik sets out the heavy metal of Brezhnev-era control: of snuffing out careers, of locking up people such as Vaclav Havel, of smudging lives.

When I secretly met the future president in Prague in 1988, he was optimistic for what tomorrow might bring. I shudder to think what Vaculik and Havel would make of Abramovich v Belton and what it portends.

Browder, too, is bleak about the impact of the case.

"I've known Catherine for many

years. She's one of the most rigorous reporters I've ever come across. I've read her book. And my own view is that the libel action against her is creating a climate of fear among journalists," he says. "You have, I believe, a bunch of oligarchs with unlimited resources who are putting all of those resources to bear to bring pressure on every other newspaper to say nothing bad about Putin's corruption.

"This is, in my opinion, not just about terrorising Catherine Belton, this is an act of terror that terrorises you and every other journalist and every other publishing company.

"And so I fear this will have a huge damping effect on vigorous reporting about what's going on in Russia, without question. And I think it goes well beyond Catherine Belton.

"And for them to do that to her, it just completely dampens any possibility of a lively debate and in my opinion, that's the purpose of this exercise."

I ask if he thinks Abramovich is an honest man?

Browder pauses. He's a lean-looking fellow who has the air of someone who can handle himself in a fight, if a fight there must be. I certainly wouldn't want to play chess with him.

"Let's put it this way," he says. "I'm not going to comment on Roman Abramovich because I don't want to be sued by him. But I would say that anybody who has become a multi-billionaire in Russia under the Putin regime has had to cut a lot of corners in order to get there. And I think there'll be very few exceptions to that rule."

But wasn't Browder just as bad as all the rest of them before finding religion?

"Well, that's an easy thing to say, except [when] you look at what I was doing in Russia.

"I was investing in big Russian companies, researching how the oligarchs who mostly controlled those companies were stealing, taking that research and publishing it, and sharing it with journalists at the Financial Times,

ABOVE: Bill Browder, pictured in 2018.

The Wall Street Journal, The New York Times and The Washington Post, and exposing the corruption.

"So I was doing just the opposite, which was trying to fix Russia. I was actually making money in the process because if you buy undervalued companies and you can expose corruption, and they stop doing the corruption, then the share price goes up."

I suggest that Navalny started out on exactly the same route, of being an angry investor.

Browder replies: "I don't want to take anything away from Alexei, not only because he's truly a legendary character. But I started what I was doing, he then emulated it."

What does Browder think of Navalny's comments in 2008, when he described most Muslim immigrants from the Caucasus as "cockroaches"? The reply is that we have all said rubbish things we later regret.

I challenge him about hiring British law firm Carter-Ruck to litigate against the Kremlin's media attack on him.

Browder defends his decision, saying "Well, I don't particularly like plaintiff libel lawyers but I hired a lawyer from Carter-Ruck to defend my rights not to be defamed by the Russian propagandists.

"There's a reason for defamation laws. They get abused often. But in this

case, the defamation laws protected me."

Looking at the long game, who is worse: Brezhnev or Putin?

"The Soviet era was bad. But they were sort of driven by ideology. With Putin, I don't believe there is any ideology. He has simply enriched himself and his friends and I believe he is driven by pure greed. So, for me, it's like having Pablo Escobar running a country that has nuclear weapons.

"I would argue that in some ways it is much more dangerous to have Vladimir Putin out there than almost any other leader you had during the Cold War; he is literally ready to do anything."

How would Browder's grandfather Earl have viewed Browder's campaign against Putin the klepto-Czar? "I hope he would have been proud of me." Those of us who worry at the ever-tightening grip of the Kremlin's dead hand on Russia – with the connivance of some in the West – could agree with that. ✖

John Sweeney is a writer and journalist who has investigated Scientology and Russian interference in the US elections. He is the host of the Hunting Ghislaine podcast

50(03):16/19|DOI:10.1177/03064220211048853

An impossible choice

Since the fall of Kabul ten days after the departure of US troops, the future of a free media, and of female journalists in particular, remains uncertain, writes **RUCHI KUMAR**

OR FIVE DAYS after the fall of Kabul to the Taliban insurgency, Mariam (not her real name) didn't leave her house. As a professional athlete, this was very unusual. However, 23-year-old Mariam is also one of the city's up and coming journalists and

staying at home did not feel right.

The militant group, known for their regressive ideology and restricting women's rights and freedoms, had forced many Afghan women to retreat into the shelter of their homes in the days following the siege. But Mariam

had enough. "I wanted to get back to work. I wanted to get out," she said.

So on Friday, an otherwise normal day off in Kabul, Mariam decided to go to her workplace, a newsroom in the centre of the city. "Around 11.45 am, as I was getting into the car, I got a call from an

unknown number. I answered it and the man on the other line, asked, 'Are you Mariam?' and I froze in my tracks."

"He sounded friendly, as though we might have been old friends," she said.

But something about his voice made her very uncomfortable. Still, she replied, "Yes I am." He then asked her, "Do you know me?" and she replied, "I don't and I don't have your number saved either. Who is this?"

Without answering her question, the man continued, this time in a much less friendly tone. "He identified the location of my office and asked if I worked there.

LEFT: A female radio critic in Afghanistan

I was so scared, I didn't reply. He then said, 'We [the Taliban] are coming for you' and I immediately hung up and put my phone on airplane mode."

Mariam is not alone.

In her short career as a journalist and TV presenter, 'Marzia' has received many threats from insurgents as well as fundamentalist groups who disapprove of her work in the media. As a woman and as a member of Afghanistan's persecuted Hazara ethnic group, she was no stranger to threats, but they were always a world away from her vibrant and empowered life in Kabul. Until, that is, the country fell into the hands of the Taliban on 15 August.

'Fauzia', another Afghan female journalist, said: "Of course there were challenges of being a journalist in Afghanistan; it was never easy. But I could deal with those because we had platforms, and more importantly, we had the media, to help us fight for our rights." Fauzia is currently on the run due to the threats she has received.

The Taliban seized control of the majority of the country earlier this month, including the capital. The Afghan president along with many top government officials were forced to flee after being asked to resign on the pretext of creating a transitional government. The militants, however, have taken control of the capital and large parts of the country creating panic and chaos among those who have been outspoken critics of the Taliban.

SINCE THE FALL, there has been a rush of Afghans trying to escape the country to avoid persecution from the Taliban who are known to be vengeful. The Journalists in Distress (JID) network, a collaborative effort of media support organisations like the Committee to Protect Journalists (CPJ) and the International Women's Media Foundation (IWMF) are working

We knew sooner or later they would come looking for us so we destroyed all our documents

in collaboration to evacuate Afghan journalists to safety.

Nadine Hoffman, deputy director of the IWMF said: "The race to evacuate Afghan media workers and their families has been the most challenging and complex emergency the press freedom community has faced. Conditions on the ground, particularly at the Hamid Karzai International Airport, have made this gargantuan task feel at times insurmountable."

"Those individuals we are supporting to evacuate have faced extreme physical duress; they have been beaten, shot at, and threatened in their homes by the Taliban. It is heartbreaking to watch this tragedy unfold. Women journalists voices in Afghanistan are being silenced."

In a statement on Monday, the CPJ shared that they had registered and vetted the cases of nearly 400 journalists in need of evacuation, and is reviewing thousands of additional requests. Other organisations have similarly large lists of media persons seeking safe passage out of Kabul.

In a press conference held the day after the fall, Taliban spokesperson Zabihullah Mujahid assured that media will remain independent but said the journalists "should not work against national values". However, despite the group's assurance of a full amnesty to those who work in media and the previous government, Afghan journalists do not trust the terror group with a history of violence against the Afghan media. ➜

→ Already, several journalists have reported being threatened by Taliban members across the country. Meanwhile, the CPJ also documented multiple attacks on the press from the Taliban, including physical attacks. A female state TV anchor was also forced off the air, underlining the Taliban's lack of commitment to protecting the rights of journalists.

Several at-risk journalists shared that the Taliban had been visiting their homes collecting information on "those who worked with infidels" and warned that action would be taken later, implying this would happen after the complete withdrawal of foreign forces from Afghanistan.

"We knew sooner or later they would come looking for us so we destroyed all our documents, certificates and IDs that show our work with the Americans," said a journalist from Nangarhar province, 'Sahar'. "It was the body of my lifetime of achievements, and I set it all on fire," she added, the grief evident in her voice.

However, it did little good, as the Taliban came to Sahar's neighbourhood armed with biometrics devices seeking to identify people with data that was shared with the previous government. "They haven't come to our house yet. I know they will kill me. They have already killed some of my friends," referring to the journalists assassinated in March in Jalalabad.

Sahar's fears are not unfounded. Taliban fighters killed the relative of a Deutsche Welle (DW) journalist on Thursday, while looking for him during a similar door-to-door search as described by Sahar. "They shot dead

ABOVE: Taliban fighters in a training camp in Faryab Province, Afghanistan

one member of his family and seriously injured another," DW reported.

In early August, unidentified gunmen shot and killed Toofan Omar, the owner of Paktia Ghag Radio. Officials in Kabul said Omar was targeted by the Taliban due to his work.

Last month, the group killed and mutilated the body of Danish Siddiqui, an Indian journalist working with Reuters, in Spin Boldak in Kandahar province.

Notably, of the total seven journalists killed in Afghanistan this year, four have been women, highlighting the increased risks women in media like Mariam, Fauzia and Sahar face. Already, earlier this year, the Afghan Journalists Safety Committee reported that nearly 20 per cent of Afghan women quit the media due to the threats they faced. The Afghan media watchdog reported that

at least nine provinces in the country had no female journalists employed in the media, essentially depriving women's voices and presence in the national debate.

These figures are feared to have risen considerably. "Soon there will be no one left to tell the story of Afghanistan," Fauzia remarked.

After the call Mariam received on Friday, she made a decision she never thought she would ever have to make. Choking back tears, she said. "I decided to leave my homeland; a country I had previously wanted to serve."

"I went back home, packed a small bag and left for the airport with my sister. We got on the first plane they [offered]. I don't even know where we are going but I know we can't live there." ✖

[All names of journalists in this article have been changed to protect their identities.]

Ruchi Kumar is an independent journalist reporting from Afghanistan and India on politics, conflict, women and development issues. She tweets as @RuchiKumar

50(03):20/22 | DOI:10.1177/03064220211048854

I went home, packed a bag and left for the airport with my sister. We got on the first plane they [offered]. I don't even know where we are going

Slightly Foxed

Words under fire

When those in power want to control access to history and ideas, libraries are often the first to be targeted, reports **RACHAEL JOLLEY**

ABOVE: The burnt remains of the Central Library at Mosul University, May 2018

"ALMOST THREE DECADES ago, some three million books and countless artefacts went up in flames when Sarajevo's National and University Library – inside the Vijecnica (city hall) – was burned to the ground. The destruction of the Vijecnica at the beginning of the war was a symbol for one of the aggressor's main objectives – silencing the soul of the city and crushing the cultural identity of an entire society."

So said Dunja Mijatović, the current Council of Europe commissioner for human rights, who was born in Sarajevo when it was part of Yugoslavia.

Just weeks before the anniversary of the burning of the library on 25 August 1992, Mijatović spoke to Index about its symbolism and what its destruction was meant to achieve.

She quoted Heinrich Heine's play, Almansor: "Where they burn books they will also, in the end, burn people."

Libraries and archives have been targets for centuries, and the reason is always the same: it's about taking away knowledge and stifling free thinking.

Libraries are, and have always been, symbols of freedom – the freedom to think and learn and find documents and books to debate and discuss.

Throughout history, when authoritarians take power and seek to control thought and behaviour, they either lock up libraries or destroy the manuscripts and books inside them.

The Serbian forces who burned the Sarajevo library were seeking to obliterate evidence of Bosnia and Herzegovina's existence as a successful multicultural and multi-ethnic state. The documents they burned told a different history from the one that the army leaders wanted to portray.

Omar Mohammed, who reported as Mosul Eye on the Isis occupation of his city in Iraq, risked his life to blog anonymously about the occupiers' wish to destroy books as well as to execute people as they sought to repress the population.

Mohammed told Index that it was not just the university library that was destroyed in Mosul, but it was the one that was reported on the most.

Many other libraries, even private collections, were wiped out. "The only possible reason is because knowledge is power," he said. "Once you prevent people from accessing knowledge then you will have full control over them."

Like many other scholars who have delved into the history of libraries, Mohammed understands that it is not about the buildings themselves.

"They don't want people to have this access because they know if people write the history, it will be completely different from the one they wanted it to be," he said.

Targeting libraries sends out a

 Where they burn books they will also, in the end, burn people

powerful message to scholars, historians and scientists, he added.

"When they see that such people are able to totally target the libraries, that they are literally able to destroy everything, it's a manifestation of brutality."

Today, Richard Ovenden, the most senior librarian at the Bodleian libraries at the University of Oxford, is worried about libraries in Turkey being closed under pressure from the government of president Recep Tayyip Erdoğan.

According to some sources, at least 188 libraries were closed there between 2002 and 2020.

Ovenden's book, Burning the Books, looks at the history of the intentional destruction of knowledge. He was recently contacted by a Turkish student, who said: "I've just read your book and I want you to know how bad it is in Turkey, because libraries are being destroyed. And all the things that you write about are true in Turkey today."

Ovenden said: "There is an absolutely authoritarian control over knowledge. Attacks on knowledge are being exercised by the authoritarian leader of Turkey right now. It is the ability for the population to generate their own ideas and to come up with their own thoughts that some governments, some authoritarian powers, some dictators and rulers do not like."

When dictatorships seek to establish that certain minorities don't exist, or haven't lived somewhere, getting rid of the documentary evidence is very convenient.

Archives that establish the existence of Uighurs in China and Muslims in parts of India also look like targets.

Ovenden feels that what is fantastically important about libraries is that they "preserve the past thoughts and ideas of human beings so they're parts of that evidence base".

He added: "They're also disseminating institutions [where] you can borrow the books, you can come and take those ideas away and write other books about them, or pamphlets,

 **When dictatorships seek to establish that certain minorities don't exist, or haven't lived somewhere, getting rid of the documentary evidence is very convenient.**

or newspaper articles, or whatever it is."

Governments around the world are failing to protect libraries as a resource, sometimes by withdrawing or drastically reducing funding.

In the UK, almost 800 libraries closed between 2010 and 2019, and a major campaign kicked off in Australia this year to save the national archives.

Michelle Arrow, professor of history at Macquarie University in Sydney, argued in April that if funding cuts were not reversed, irreplaceable audio-visual collections would fall apart. After a public campaign, the national government has delivered some extra funding, but this has not solved all the archives' problems.

She told Index that with a reduction in staff of almost 25% since 2013, more staff would be needed to deal with the large backlog of requests to view archived material.

She said the archives contained "unique records, and they touch almost every Australian: it is a democratic archive, a collection of ordinary people's records, rather than famous or renowned Australians".

While some countries are seeing numerous library closures due to financial or other threats, there are new defenders coming to light. In the coastal city of Santa Cruz in California, there's a massive investment in upgrades to current libraries, and new ones are opening over the next two years.

Santa Cruz mayor Donna Meyers told Index: "In California, we just tend to believe in public institutions. We believe that public education, public libraries, all of that, lead to a better community, lead to a more informed society."

Santa Cruz residents passed a special tax – by 78% of the vote – to pay for investment in the libraries which, Meyers says, is a sign of how committed the community is to libraries being around for future generations.

Back in Sarajevo, Mijatović can see the new library that rose from the ashes of the Vijecnica from her terrace.

She said: "One hopes that the soul and the people of Sarajevo will recover and that new generations will hopefully enjoy this magnificent symbol of Sarajevo and, more importantly, live in peace." ✖

Rachael Jolley is a contributing editor to Index and a research fellow at the Centre for the Freedom of the Media at Sheffield University.

50(03):24/25|DOI:10.1177/03064220211048855

Library destruction in recent history

1914: German troops destroy the library of the Catholic University of Louvain

1939: The Great Talmudic Library in Lublin is destroyed by the Nazis

1966-76: Chairman Mao destroys libraries across China as part of the Cultural Revolution

1976-79: The Khmer Rouge deliberately destroy libraries across Cambodia, including the Phnom Penh national library

2013: Islamic troops set fire to the library in Timbuktu, Mali

Letters from Lukashenka's prisoners

Our new campaign shares correspondence from political prisoners being held in Belarus

N A HIGHLY disputed election in August 2020 in Belarus, incumbent president Alyaksandr Lukashenka claimed victory to begin a sixth term in office. Lukashenka, often known as Europe's last dictator, has been in power since 1994.

Following the election, protests erupted and a vicious crackdown ensued. A year on from the election, there are more than 600 political prisoners in the country.

Letters from Lukashenka's Prisoners is a collaborative project by Index on Censorship in partnership with Belarus Free Theatre, Human Rights House Foundation and Politzek.

The campaign gives unjustly detained individuals a voice by collecting, translating, and publishing their letters in Index on Censorship magazine and weekly on our website. The letters are heart-rending and show the real people behind the grim statistic. ✖

Read letters each week from Lukashenka's prisoners at indexoncensorship.org/lukashenkaletters

50(03):26/31|DOI:10.1177/03064220211048856

Volha Takarchuk, political vlogger

VOLHA TAKARCHUK runs a political vlog with almost 37,000 subscribers. She was detained several times after the August 2020 election, but on the morning of 19 May her apartment was searched, some of her belongings were seized, and she was detained. She has remained in prison since then.

WHEN VOLHA'S PARENTS tried to deliver a food package to her on 8 June, they were told that she had been placed in solitary confinement for allegedly violating the "rules of procedure". They were not told what the alleged violation was. In her letter below, Volha refers to the effects that her "lockup" had on her.

She is writing to one of her supporters, Elena. Volha's reference to having received a "parrot – Dracula and BMW" are understood to be a response to the contents of Elena's letter. She also refers to her two young children, who she says she cannot bear to be without. By now, she has already missed both of their birthdays.

Letter

Elena, hello. I received your parrot – Dracula and the BMW :) Thank you, it was very interesting to read all that. At least it distracted me a little from my bad thoughts.

I'm doing so-so. I've been transferred to another cell, the same one I was in the first days I spent here! The girls here are much nicer than in my previous cell, so it's easier to be here. There are a lot of people here older than myself, so they help me out and look out for me. But somehow it doesn't really help. The days pass and nothing changes. At least, the lack of news makes it feel that way.

My lawyer said again that if they don't extend the investigation, (and God forbid they don't), then the trial will only happen, at the earliest, in mid-August, what with all this rigmarole. Which means I won't be able to make it to the kids' birthdays. Matvei will be 8 on 5 August , and A will be 4. That's what I'm going through. I just keep crying and crying. No sedatives help.

Other than that, things are improving here. During the heatwave, I was pretty ill. And the consequences of incarceration were taking their toll. My blood pressure skyrocketed, my head was aching, and I was constantly dizzy. I was so weak that I couldn't stand. I had a terrible earache another day.

Now I'm doing better. I was prescribed pills for the blood pressure, and they put absorbent cotton wool with alcohol in my ear. :) Overall, I'll live.

I'm constantly praying that they let me go home from the trial. I can't bear to be without my children anymore. I'm at the end of my tether. I read all the time to distract myself. And wait for night to come, so I can go to bed. Before I fall asleep I think of Lolita's song: "One more agonising day will come and go, I'll want to live…"

I keep waiting for the day when I want to live again. You wrote that I need to smile. I know that, but it's just so hard here. Everything has become meaningless without the children, life is miserable, and there is nothing positive at all!!! So even with joy and a smile, I'm still having a dreadful time. There's no clear mirror here (probably a good thing), but what I can see in the one we've got scares me. My eyes are grey, lifeless, completely empty. My skin is grey, and the bags under my eyes almost reach my chin!

I'd terrify you :) But, unfortunately, that's just the way things are. Write to me. And thanks for all your support!

Hugs, Volha

Aliaksandr Vasilevich, businessman

ALIAKSANDR VASILEVICH is a businessman, owner of the Vondel/Hepta advertising agency and the "Ў" Gallery, which was formerly one of the main cultural centres in Belarus. He is also the co-founder of the online media outlets Kyky.org and TheVillage Belarus. He was detained on 28 August 2020 and charged on 4 September 2020. However, his lawyer has been prohibited from disclosing information about the investigation, so the charges against him remain unknown.

ALIAKSANDR HAS TWO daughters. Below is an example of the stories he has been writing in letters to his eldest daughter, Adelia, who is eight years old. His second daughter, Urshula (referred to in the letter as "Ursh") was born while he was in detention so he hasn't met her yet. The stories below were sent in three separate letters between May and July 2021.

PAPA AND THE PENGUIN, OR, HOW TO STAY SANE IN PRISON

Papa was sitting in his cell, drinking coffee and eating chocolate cake. His friends had given him the cake and it was delicious. And Daddy simply loved coffee.

The door opened, and in walked Penguin with a mattress in one hand and bag in the other. The door slammed shut behind him. Penguin looked exhausted and dishevelled. "Hello," he said. "Hi there!" said Papa in reply, as he showed Penguin where to put his mattress and his belongings.

After drinking his tea, Penguin sat on the bed and looked at Papa.

"Why are you so calm and not miserable? After all, you and I have had a bad run of luck. It was all fine, and now it's terrible :("

Papa smiled at the Penguin. "And if it was never bad, how would you know when it was good? Unfortunate things happen to everyone. Even in cartoons. Even to princesses and villains. To good people and bad people."

Penguin looked even sadder. "Sure, sure, sure. But you're not sad?"

Papa took a gulp of coffee and said: "Why should I be? I'm here, in prison. I can't change that or influence the situation. But I can choose to be sad or happy. I have power over myself. What would you choose – to be sad or happy? Or at least calm."

Penguin responded without thinking: "Of course, I'd choose to be happy, or at least calm. But how?"

"Have you been happy before? Told jokes? Played? Read books? Chatted with your friends? Watched cartoons? Played games?"

"Yeah…" muttered Penguin.

"That's how you stay cheerful, don't let yourself be changed. Keep being just the way you like to be."

"But I'm prison, aren't I!?" said Penguin.

"Yeah, so what? Right now, we're sitting and having a chat. Right this second. Are you enjoying our conversation?"

"It's better than thinking about how bad I feel. I'm enjoying it."

"So you're feeling okay now?"

"Mm-hmm. Probably, I guess, but later…"

"There isn't a later! Think about now! Enjoy every moment. Look, here's a low-calorie biscuit."

"It gets better!" said Penguin, munching on the biscuit.

"And you can create even more little pleasures; think on them and concentrate on them," said Daddy, as he took a biscuit himself. The last biscuit of the day.

"Do I have to eat biscuits all the time?" Penguin wondered. "Won't I get fat? That's unhealthy."

Daddy smiled. "Read if you enjoy it. Get to know the people around you. Treat them the way you want to be treated. Make jokes. Write letters to your friends."

"But I want to play on my iPad."

"Well, you don't have an iPad. So choose. Do you want to sit there all miserable, or would you prefer to read an interesting book?"

"A boooook!" shouted Penguin, as he flapped his wings.

"Here you go." Papa had taken a book out from under his mattress.

ABOVE: Adelia's penguin

Penguin read the title: Papa and Penguin!

Adelia, hi. If you liked this story, please draw the penguin :) I love you and miss you so much.

Dad

PENGUIN'S WINGS

Wheezing, panting, grunting, groaning…

"Breathe in, breathe out." Penguin was doing rhythmic push-ups. His right wing and leg were on the bed on the right; his left wing and leg were on the bed on the left. As he breathed in, Penguin lowered himself below the second tier of the bunk beds, hovering at a height of just under two meters. The grey and yellow walls of the cell flashed before his eyes like a reproduction of Kazimir's Malevich's 'Red Cavalry Riding' and a boring programme on TV. Penguin liked to work out on the second level of the bunk beds – the cell was cramped, with 12 prisoners aside from him in the room, which was slightly bigger than a child's room.

> *The cement walls are in bad condition, and there's a lattice overhead, and a few green leaves higher up along the walls. Sometimes good things can grow, even in cement.*

"200," exhaled Penguin. "And tomorrow, I'll do push-ups, and after that, bar work."

"You're doing a great job," said Papa. "You'll be the first jock-penguin :)"

"A gym bunny!" the others joked.

During their assigned walking time, Penguin and Papa paced nonstop from wall to wall. To the guards above, they must have looked like zombies flailing around the little courtyard in desperation :) The cement walls are in bad condition, and there's a lattice overhead, and a few green leaves higher up along the walls. Sometimes good things can grow, even in cement.

"I wish I could make my wings big enough to fly," Penguin said dreamily as they reached their ten-thousandth step. Papa remained tactfully silent as a response. He turned his face up towards the sun's rays which had made their way through the lattice.

"I know I can't fly. But I won't crawl either," Penguin continued.

"You'll get better. And movement and improvement make life better," answered Papa.

In the evening, lying on his bed before going to sleep, Papa decided to continue: "It's like with goodness and light. Darkness and boredom all around. But you're doing something good. Even a little thing. Acts of kindness. And the light gets stronger. The world changes. Even if the change is not as quick as everyone would like."

"Is that how you build a nest out of a bunch of tiny useless pebbles?" Penguin was asking for clarification.

"Sort of :)" grunted Papa, and he fell asleep.

A few days later, a neighbour approached Papa and Penguin, who were doing some intense push-ups and panting heavily.

"Can I try?"

"Of course."

The neighbour climbed up and, panting even more vigorously than Papa and Penguin, was only able to do five push-ups.

"Don't worry, don't give up! Try to do more, and you'll be able to do even more than me," Penguin encouraged his neighbour, who was bright red, and dripping with sweat. After a couple of weeks, more than half the cell had started to join in on their workouts.

The neighbour, Papa, and Penguin were drinking coffee. The neighbour was chewing on an unsweetened, but still tasty biscuit, given to Papa by his mother-in-law. "I haven't done anything in 10 years. And today I feel better. I wrote a letter to my son, telling him I'd started working out," recounted the neighbour contentedly. "I should take up English too."

The sadness seemed to clear a little. The bleak wasted time was gone. But Penguin still couldn't fly. Penguins can't fly. Another month passed. Penguin's term had been extended by two months. He climbed up the bunk beds. "I'm going to do 300 push-ups," he thought. And when half of his cellmates, who had been taking their turns to do their own push-ups with him, finally decided to rest, one of his new friends said: "I heard you want to fly. When we get out of here, you can come to me. I'll teach you how to fly a glider. And then maybe you can learn to fly a plane. You're a persistent guy."

THE PENGUIN AND THE FRAME

"What shall we have with our tea?" asked Penguin.

"Hmmm…. Biscuits or chocolate brownies?" asked Papa.

"What's healthier?" asked Penguin, with a sigh, as he looked at his waist.

"Well, cookies are 10% unhealthy, and brownies are 90% healthy," laughed Papa.

"Brownies, then!" His companion was decisive.

Papa let him enjoy the moment. And when Penguin reached for a second piece of brownie, he asked him: "Why did you choose the brownie?"

"It's healthy!"

"Don't you know that 10% unhealthy and 90% healthy mean the same thing?"

"Oops. How did that happen?"

"You fell for the framing effect. It's an effect of formulation. Often our decision is a result not of what we want, what is correct, or what we like more, but how the question is asked.

"So what do we do, how do we not get caught in that trap?"

"Be careful and think :) So you don't get manipulated."

"Can I have a biscuit? I prefer them."

"Of course, here you are. And I like brownies more."

"And what are we having for lunch?"

"A salad. 100% healthy. :)"

"Great! I'm getting sick of these biscuits. :)" The End.

ABOVE: Aliaksandr Vasilevich

Adelia, hi!

Check out the new story :) Have a great time celebrating your mum's birthday. I love you and miss you a lot. Hugs! And give Ursh a hug too!

Dad

Maxim Znak, lawyer

MAXIM ZNAK is a lawyer who has been in detention since 18 September 2020. Shortly after his detention he told his lawyer: "Normal life of society is impossible without law, just as human life is impossible without food". He has now been sentenced to ten years in jail.

IN MAY 2020, Maxim joined the team of opposition figure and then presidential nominee Viktar Babaryka to provide legal assistance to his team. Maxim later represented Sviatlana Tsikhanouskaya and Maria Kalesnikava, with whom he has since stood trial. He faces up to 12 years in prison on charges of calling for "actions aimed at causing harm to the national security of the Republic of Belarus."

While in prison Maxim has been writing and sending poems to his family. In November 2020, a poem he sent to his father, Alisksandr Znak, was almost completely censored by the authorities.

In July 2021, he wrote the poem translated below.

16 July 2021
Shame
It's despicable to judge in secret.
It's low. Embarrassing. And indecent.

Did I call publicly? To revolt? I?
At least accuse me publicly.
Conspiracy? With whom, how and when?
Why a secret trial in another house?
A secret trial is forever:
That kind of thing doesn't sink in the
Summer, either.
An extremist group? That's a lie!
Unless the ghost of the bloody Troika
And, hiding his name,
An expert in black balaclava shame.

It worked. Here I have already mastered many allied professions. I can't say that something is a vocation, but it's certainly interesting to live in. So, like the classic – to struggle and to seek, to find and not to give up! By the way, mining mechanical engineers are very cool in all the cool fantasy books. They're gnomes ;) Do! Hi all!

Maxim Znak

> *Did I call publicly? To revolt? I? At least accuse me publicly. Conspiracy? With whom, how and when?*

Maria Kalesnikava, musician and political activist

In September 2020, the prominent Belarusian opposition figure **MARIA KALESNIKAVA** was abducted from Minsk and taken to the border where security forces tried to expel her from the country; she ripped up her passport in defiance. In the days that followed she was charged with incitement to undermine national security and placed in pre-trial detention. In early September, Maria was sentenced to 11 years in prison.

THE LETTER THAT follows was written by Maria Kalesnikova to her father on 16 July 2021, the day the Supreme Court rejected her complaint regarding the extension of her detention until 1 August.

Her father, Aliaksandr Kalesnikov, had gone to the hearing to support his daughter wearing a T-shirt with Maria's image on it (pictured right). He was initially refused access to the hearing so he took off the T-shirt, turned

BELOW: Maria Kalesnikava

it inside out, and put it back on. He was then allowed to enter.

Aliaksandr has repeatedly been refused the right to visit Maria in detention. According to Maria's sister, Tatsiana Khomich – referred to as "Tania" in the letter, Aliaksandr has been denied permission to see his daughter on every occasion (more than fifteen times) with no explanation. On 4 August, Maria went on trial facing up to 12 years in prison on charges of extremism. The trial was closed to the public, including family members. Maria's family said it was a relief to see her healthy and cheerful at the trail, albeit on television screens.

Tatsiana said that although Maria is writing a lot, her letters have become increasingly infrequent. Suppression of letters from political prisoners in Belarus is commonplace, denying family members and loved ones the chance to hear vital news. This is done to put pressure on individuals and their families. The letter below is the last communication Maria's family have received from her. One year since the fraudulent elections in Belarus, Maria's sister agreed to publicly share this personal letter.

ABOVE: Kalesnikava (left) has been sentenced to 11 years in prison and Znak (right) ten

Letter from Maria Kalesnikava to her father Aliaksandr Kalesnikov:
16 July 2021:

Hi my dearly beloved world's best dad!

How are you doing in this trying time?

I'm constantly thinking of you, grandpa and all our nearest and dearest – sending my hello's and lots of hugs to all!

The court hearing took place today so I already know how you had to 'get changed' – I bet everybody in the detention centre could hear me laugh! You really think fast on your feet. You see, now nobody can doubt that I'm my father's daughter – and I'm so proud to be one!

I'm so glad that you are keeping your spirits high and are managing to get through these crazy days with a good sense of humour :)

Keep it up!

Today I received two! Letters from you and two from A.

You wrote that you're in awe of Tania – I'm also writing this in every letter to her. What she's doing for me and our whole team is unbelievable and incredible.

Please ask her, as do I, to make sure that she takes good care of herself and makes every effort to find time to rest.

And of course, the joke that your Berlingo [car] is crumbling and ageing faster than you are has also put a smile on my face. And so it should be, Dad, you've got no need to crumble!

I'm well, healthy and cheerful!

Sending you and everybody a big-big hug!

Your Masha
May goodness persevere!
Love and hugs

The court hearing took place today so I already know how you had to 'get changed' – I bet everybody in the detention centre could hear me laugh! You really think fast on your feet.

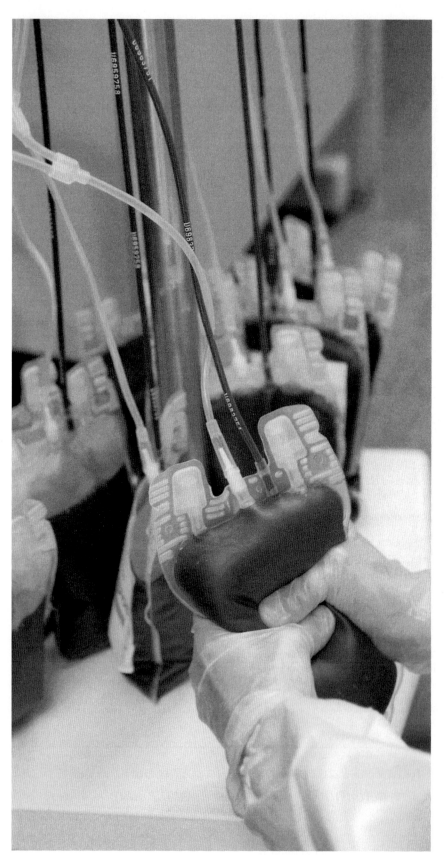

Bad blood

KELLY DUDA travelled to Italy to offer his services as a prosecution witness in a trial about blood contamination but now faces charges himself

S I WAS looking at possible photos to accompany this piece, it triggered a flashback…

It's 2 December 2017. I'm on a red-eye from Los Angeles to Rome. After years of email exchanges, Stefano Bertone, an Italian attorney, has asked me to testify in a criminal trial in Naples. Despite the inevitable wear and tear of long-distance travel and the economic burden of not being paid for my time, I want to help. So I have agreed.

The defendants, Duilio Poggiolini, the former head of the pharmaceutical department of the ministry of health, who'd been previously convicted of taking millions in bribes from Big Pharma, and 10 representatives of the Marcucci Group – an Italian drug company and fractionator – are being tried on manslaughter charges for supplying Italians with blood products that were tainted with HIV and viral hepatitis, resulting in illness and death.

"Fractionation" refers to the general processes by which blood plasma proteins are separated into different blood products, including anticoagulants to treat haemophiliacs. A total of 2,605 Italian haemophiliacs were infected in the 1980s and 1990s with HIV and hepatitis from contaminated blood products.

Because of my work as an investigative reporter in the USA exposing the Arkansas prison blood scandal, and my subsequent documentary, Factor 8, I had valuable information for the prosecution.

For three decades, the state of Arkansas profited from blood collected from prisoners at the Cummins Unit facility. From 1978 until 1985, Health Management Associates (HMA), founded by Dr Francis "Bud" Henderson, ran the plasma programme for the state. Inmates were paid peanuts to give blood twice a week – blood that was sold on the global market. HMA and the state pocketed millions. There was but one major problem: disease.

Many of the state's inmates were infected with viral hepatitis and HIV/Aids. As a result, thousands of unwitting victims in countries worldwide, including Italy, received medications made from this contaminated source and died as a result.

On the 14-hour flight, I don't eat and can't sleep. From the airport, it's a 90-minute train ride to Naples. After exiting Piazza Garibaldi and using my Google Maps app to find our hotel, out of nowhere a figure rushes me and violently snatches my smartphone, running off down a dark, rainswept alley.

The next morning, after still not having eaten anything, my partner Sarah and I head to a small press conference where I meet reporters and one of the victims. Together, we walk to the courthouse, which looks like a post-World War II Soviet Union building.

Once inside, we're surprised to realise there's no heat. Inside the courtroom, the chairs are threadbare. A reporter greets me in English: "Welcome to Hell" – not exactly what I'm expecting. Meanwhile, the defence side of the room is filled with corporate lawyers, grinning and yucking it up, without a care in the world.

Before the proceedings start, Sarah uses my SLR camera to record some video footage. Two weeks earlier, we'd been given permission to shoot my testimony. However, within minutes, the defence objects and the prosecutor, Lucio Giugliano, doesn't push back. So the judge, Antonio Palumba, orders us to stop filming. Bertone turns to me and says in English: "He [Giugliano] doesn't

ABOVE: Duda's comments enraged the Italian prosecutor

want the world to know what's going on in his courtroom today." You can imagine my surprise.

Bertone and Ermanno Zancla are acting as civil attorneys for the victims who are attached to the prosecution, which is allowed in Italy. Both have successfully represented tainted blood victims in other civil proceedings, and over the course of many years have been able to build a criminal case for this prosecution.

(There's no jury, and criminal trials can last for years, which allowed Guelfo Marcucci, known as the "father of Italian fractionation", to escape final prosecution before his death in 2015. He denied using prison blood from the USA in blood products.)

A reporter greets me in English: 'Welcome to Hell' – not exactly what I'm expecting

The drug company's lawyers object to me testifying, and again Giugliano rolls over. But this time, Bertone vigorously counters the objections. What's going on? I've flown across the Atlantic, and I'm jet-lagged, hungry, sleep-deprived, not getting paid and have already lost my cell phone – and all for this?

My interpreter, whom Bertone has hired out of his own pocket, tries to translate as the lawyers continue arguing. After a lot of back and forth, the judge rules that I will testify. Phew.

But now the defence objects to any of my recorded interviews from my documentary being used as evidence. This time Giugliano jumps out of his seat and agrees with them. This evidence is crucial as it will provide the link between the Cummins Unit in Lincoln County, Arkansas, and Italy. Why is the prosecutor siding with the drug company's lawyers?

After another lengthy debate, the judge decides that he'll make his ruling after hearing my testimony. I would find out later that Giugliano had already told Bertone that he could see no connection to Arkansas. What he really meant was that he didn't want to see any connection. →

→ As things progress, it's Bertone, not the prosecutor, who asks me questions. As we destroy the defence's case, point by point, the smiles on the faces of the defence attorneys disappear. At various points, Giugliano tries to block Bertone's line of questioning but is overruled by the judge.

Through my testimony, I'm able to establish that 1) the blood from Arkansas was known to come from a high-risk prison population; 2) US state and federal health officials, as well as Big Pharma, knew there had been severe regulatory problems with the Cummins blood programme; and 3) tainted blood from Cummins was exported to Italy and was even subject to two unsuccessful US Food and Drug Administration (FDA) recalls in August 1983.

Finally, at the end of more than four hours of testimony, Giugliano decides to ask me a few questions, all designed to discredit me. He fails.

The judge decides he wants to watch an excerpt of my interview with Henderson of HMA. In the clip, Henderson explains that after the recalls, he'd travelled with officials to Rieti, Italy – the headquarters of AIMA Plasmaderivati, the processing plant for Marcucci's only fractionation centre for its haemophilia treatment products. The clip is played for the entire courtroom. The reporters are stunned.

Next, I submit a letter in which Henderson admits that HMA paid a $250,0000 settlement as a result of the recalls.

Though exhausted, I prepare myself for a tough cross-examination. To my surprise, the defence attorneys pose only two questions.

The first attempts to establish that very little was known about the health hazards of blood-borne diseases at the time of the recalls in late 1983. However, I inform them that in the USA, health officials knew in the 1960s that prisoners were at high risk for having viral hepatitis, and that high levels of liver enzymes were present in 30 to 60%

I'm confused. I assume this is some kind of wounded ego thing – until I see the back door open and the police coming for me

of the prison population. In December of 1982, because of the growing Aids crisis, the FDA asked US fractionators to exclude plasma collected at prisons.

The second question attempts to assert that there was no test for hepatitis C or HIV at the time. I assure them that surrogate tests for antibodies and surface antigen tests of hepatitis B were used by the industry in screening blood. Also, researchers knew that previous exposure to hepatitis-B was considered a significant indication of possible infection with Aids. So if you failed either test, you were automatically disqualified.

However, because the Cummins blood programme was often run by inmates, there were always ways to get around the rules and fake the test results, if an infected inmate wanted to donate.

After that, the defence folds. Game over. Or so I believe…

As the proceedings come to a close, I ask Bertone, the first lawyer for the victims, if I can speak to the prosecutor. With his assurance that it's OK, I ask the interpreter to accompany me. Sarah, camera in hand, follows.

As we approach the table, Giugliano sticks out his hand. I shake it and tell him: "In my country, what you did today as a prosecutor would be disgraceful." He pauses and then yells at the judge. He exclaims to the court that I have just committed a crime and that he wants me arrested.

I'm confused. I assume this is some kind of wounded ego thing – until I see the back door open and the police coming for me. Apparently, I'm now being accused of multiple crimes.

Meanwhile, the defence attorneys spot Sarah shooting the video, so they want her thrown in jail, too. The police seize my passport and order Sarah to

delete video files off her camera. It's sheer chaos. A lot of confusion. A lot of shouting in Italian.

By now, Bertone and Zancla have become my defence attorneys against the prosecution. I feel like I've entered The Twilight Zone as the prosecutor is trying to jail his own witness – me.

Eventually the judge rules in my favour – I'm not going to prison. However, I'm still detained and questioned further by the police. I'm forced to secure legal representation while in Italy in case the authorities come back for me.

By now, the sun has set. It's dark outside. And I still haven't eaten…

The next day, Bertone and Zancla ask for Giuliano to be sanctioned and "replaced by a magistrate who really plays the role of the prosecution". Giuliano is not removed.

Fast-forward to 19 April 2019. Three weeks after the Court of Naples finds the defendants not guilty, I am informed that I've been under criminal investigation in Rome for the past eight months. On 13 November, I'm further notified that I will be tried under two indictments in a criminal court in Rome beginning on 11 December on the charges of "outrage", of violating penal code 343, and of offending the honour or prestige of a magistrate, punishable with up to three years in prison.

It turns out that not only do the Marcuccis have a considerable business empire made up of pharmaceutical companies such as Kedrion, with a marketplace in 100 countries including the USA, but they have deep political ties to the Italian government with Senator Andrea Marcucci (son of Guelfo) being close friends with former health minister Francesco De Lorenzo. He was once considered the right-hand man to former prime minister Matteo Renzi.

The Marcuccis are also known for threatening journalists with lawsuits, and tried to force one of the few reporters at my hearing, Andrea Cinquegrani, to remove his online coverage for The Voice by threatening legal action.

My case is indicative of a general campaign against journalists in Italy.

The use of criminal lawsuits and strategic lawsuits against public participation (SLAPPs) against the media in Italy has been described by the European Centre for Press and Media Freedom as a "daily emergency for journalists". In addition, 21 Italian journalists are currently under round-the-clock police protection because of serious threats or murder attempts by the mafia and other criminal organisations.

Regular citizens' rights to freedom of speech also must be upheld and cannot be threatened by the misuse of the penal code. As the Italian Supreme Court has previously ruled, magistrates are not immune to criticism or questioning.

After two delays during the coronavirus pandemic, my criminal trials are set to begin next January. Three reporters' rights groups will be helping me with my defence: Media Defence, Free Press Unlimited and Ossigeno per l'Informazione.

Innocent Italians were poisoned by dirty prison blood from the USA. Seeking justice for them, I travelled a long way to share my testimony.

The guilty went free but now I'm facing jail time. How is this justice?

I look forward to my day in court to prove that you can't get away with burying the truth by retaliating against journalists. ✖

ABOVE: Filmmaker and activist Kelly Duda

Kelly Duda is an activist and producer and director of the documentary Factor 8: The Arkansas Prison Blood Scandal

Asked for his response to Duda's article, the prosecutor in the case, Lucio Giugliano, told

Index on Censorship in mid-September: "In the Italian legal system, it is the only the public prosecutor who may maintain 'personally, or through a specifically delegated magistrate of the office, relations with the media', and 'it is forbidden for the magistrates of the public prosecutor to issue statements or provide information to the media about the judicial activity of the office'. Therefore, in spite of myself, I am not authorised to make any statement on the matter."

50(03):32/35|DOI:10.1177/03064220211048857

≡ 21 Italian journalists are under police protection because of serious threats or murder attempts by the mafia.

LEFT: Prisoners released from Insein Prison on the outskirts of Yangon, Myanmar, after being set free on general amnesty in May 2011. Then president Thein Sein had announced the amnesty for more than 14,600 inmates across the country on state TV the previous day. It is now home once more to opponents of the military junta.

Welcome to Hell

Filled with people jailed for doing their jobs, Myanmar's Insein prison is a place to be feared. **BENJAMIN LYNCH** hears about its horrors from a former inmate

IMAGINE LIFE LOCKED in a room with people who want to harm you.

Picture it as dank and dark, with near inedible food, a place where the people keeping you in there can abuse you at any moment.

Hell on Earth might just be Myanmar's Insein prison.

Situated in the country's most populous city, Yangon, Insein has been a favourite of regimes to punish political activists and dissidents. Ousted leader Aung San Suu Kyi was imprisoned there.

Since the coup of 1 February, Insein has become the home for yet more journalists and activists who are there merely for doing their jobs – be it reporting on acts of brutality by the military or the number of deaths or, in

the case of one former detainee who spoke to Index, taking photographs (which are shown over the following pages). Ye Myo Khant was arrested earlier this year while covering a protest.

"The interior is painted light blue and the ceiling is painted green with a hint of horror. The exterior walls are painted white, and the doors are painted white," he said.

"The smell is nauseating with the sweat of people. We were uncomfortable and there are concerns about suicide.

The smell makes you choke."

His story is not uncommon. As of 6 September – according to Reporting ASEAN – 98 people working as journalists in the country have been arrested. Forty are still detained.

Early July saw a brief period of hope when around 2,000 people, including journalists, were released. Some 700 of them were reported to be from Insein prison.

But for those still detained across the country, life behind bars has remained an unjust tragedy.

There are few photos of the inside of Insein, but it is known to be stiflingly hot, cramped and unhygienic.

Overcrowding is a problem, and with well over 10,000 people reported to be contained within its walls, it houses more than double its official capacity of 5,000.

Political prisoners are not separated from those jailed for heinous crimes, and it leads to threats and intimidation which are not stamped out by the prison guards. Prisoners are, in fact, reminded by guards that harm can come to them at any time.

"We had to live in a big prison room with probably 400 detainees," said Ye Myo Khant. "We don't even get our own space. I could not sleep throughout the night and I missed my home.

"In my mind I was thinking, 'I am not a criminal. Why did they arrest us? I am just doing my work as a photojournalist'."

He said he felt that his life was in danger, adding: "In the prison there are

 There are no human rights, no humanity and no empathy

no human rights, no humanity and no empathy. I saw that the other detainees were abused by sexual harassment, beating and other types of bullying.

"I was threatened many times."

The ordeal for those detained in the prison is both physical and mental. On 23 July, a brief strike (which unconfirmed reports suggest was dealt with severely) by political prisoners was called to protest, in part, the conditions in the jail but also the lack of medical assistance.

Covid-19 in Myanmar was and is rife and quickly spread through Insein, reflecting the junta's inability to control the spread of the virus. The UN has voiced concerns that half the country's population of about 54 million people could be infected, turning the country into a "super-spreader state".

There is little to no access to oxygen or proper medical equipment, and vaccination rates are low. Queues of desperate people hoping to refill oxygen bottles can be up to 12 hours long.

A number of prisoners have died as a result, including the politician Nyan Win.

He was Aung San Suu Kyi's lawyer in 2009 when she faced five years in prison and, more recently, one of her senior legal advisers.

He joined the National League for Democracy, the party in power before this year's coup, in 1988 – shortly after it was formed – and became a key part of its pro-democracy movement. Over the course of his life he was arrested and detained several times, but his belief in democracy for Myanmar remained undeterred.

Nyan Win befriended Ye Myo Khant in Insein and offered words of guidance, speaking of his past experience of being detained and tortured by the military juntas that have ruled over the years.

Ye Myo Khant recalled: "He was tortured during his previous imprisonment. He recounted torture in that prison, interrogation, and even worse times. 'I wish you all good health and we will one day be free, and we will work for the restoration of democracy in

The odds are stacked against journalists, activists and dissidents from the start.

Myanmar,' he told me."

"He would say, 'The military council cannot detain me for my whole life, and I will be released one day'. [With other imprisoned politicians] we discussed Myanmar and talked about how to fight the dictatorship and how to build the future of Myanmar. Now that I am out, I will continue participating in the revolution [calling] for democracy in Myanmar. I remember Nyan Win's words and I am sorry that he passed away."

While the elder statesmen of the pro-democracy movement may offer words of encouragement, hope – understandably – is hard to come by in Insein. The odds are stacked against journalists, activists and dissidents from the very start. Legislative changes have made sure dissent is easily punished.

Myanmar's penal code previously made it a crime to publish or circulate any "statement, rumor or report" "with intent to cause, or which is likely to cause, any officer, soldier, sailor or airman, in the Army, Navy or Air Force to mutiny or otherwise disregard or fail in his duty."

It has been replaced with much broader language clearly designed to penalise those encouraging members of the civil service of the security services to join the Civil Disobedience Movement.

Under the revised provision, any attempt to "hinder, disturb, damage the motivation, discipline, health and conduct" of the military personnel and government employees and cause their hatred, disobedience or disloyalty toward the military and the government is punishable by up to three years in prison.

Because of the country's prohibitive laws, criticism of the regime is impossible to get away with. By their very nature, protests are critical of the regime and coverage of them is seen by the authorities as a mouthpiece for dissent.

Many reporters have fled the country and now that reporting is so clearly viewed as an act of revolution, it is up to journalists to weigh up the threats versus their own ideals.

Ye Myo Khant said: "[These journalists say] 'it is not convenient for me to live in this country. There is no law and justice for journalists. I can be rearrested at any time. I really want to be a journalist [and cover] the crimes of the coup in this country. If I cannot live in this country at all, I will have to move to another country for my work'."

Indeed, he has not been active since his release. Prior threats of intimidation towards his family are cause for concern and they have had to move to a safer location within the country.

"When I come back one day, I want to take pictures of the injustices of the military," he said. "I would like to treat my parents and family and travel with them. Of course, I completely miss my home."

Myanmar's crisis looks as though it is set to get worse, however. Prisoners returning from Insein are being released into a country in chaos. As the regime struggles to deal with Covid-19 outbreaks, civil war is also on the cards. The National Unity government's armed wing, the People's Defence Force, is reportedly attempting to unify various civil militias and armed resistance groups.

It is incumbent on the international community not to forget about Myanmar when their attention is focused elsewhere to ensure those detained are set free. ✖

Benjamin Lynch is the Tim Hetherington Fellow and editorial assistant at Index on Censorship

50(03):36/41|DOI:10.1177/03064220211048858

Myanmar: A country in turmoil

Reportage from the protests by photojournalist **YE MYO KHANT**

ABOVE: A man filming a violent crackdown by police near the Hledan Center in Yangon. 26 February 2021.

TOP-LEFT: A mass gathering in Yangon, 17 February.

LEFT: The junta's police forces block demonstrators near the American Center, 22 February.

BOTTOM-LEFT: Outside the HQ of the National League for Democracy, Aung San Suu Kyi's party, 15 February.

ABOVE: A woman protesting at the Indonesian embassy, Yangon, 21 February.

LEFT: A girl protesting with her dog near the Hleden Center, Yangon, 8 February.

TOP RIGHT: People carrying the coffin of Tin Htut Hein, a volunteer guard for a neighbourhood watch group who was shot and killed. The group was set up to address fears that the regime was using newly released criminals to terrorise citizens. 20 February.

RIGHT: Police forces block protests near the University of Yangon. 7 February..

Jennings

Our cartoonist considers whether it is always necessary to offer a right of reply in order to achieve a balanced debate

50(03):42/43|DOI:10.1177/03064220211048859

BALANCED DEBATE

BY BEN JENNINGS

GOOD EVENING — TONIGHT WE BEGIN BY SPEAKING TO SOMEONE WHO HAS STARTED A BREAKFAST CLUB FOR SCHOOLS IN THEIR LOCAL AREA THAT NOT ONLY MAKES SURE CHILDREN START THE DAY WITH A MEAL BUT ALSO TEACHES THEM ABOUT COOKING AND NUTRITION...

THANK YOU FOR JOINING US, SALLY. OF COURSE, WE COULDN'T JUST HAVE YOU ON WITHOUT ALSO INCLUDING AN OPPOSING VIEW TO YOUR FEEDING CHILDREN INITIATIVE...

TO DISCUSS THIS, WE'RE ALSO JOINED BY SATAN FROM THE CENTRE-RIGHT THINKTANK: 'THE INSTITUTE FOR EVIL ENDEAVOR AND ETERNAL DAMNATION'. THANK YOU FOR JOINING US, SATAN

PLEASSSSURE TO BE HERE

BEN JENNINGS: an award-winning cartoonist for The Guardian and The Economist whose work has been exhibited around the world

'**Extremely important and profoundly disturbing**'
ARCHBISHOP DESMOND TUTU

Do Not Disturb

'A withering assault on the murderous Rwandan regime of Paul Kagame – very driven, very impassioned'
JOHN LE CARRÉ

'An extremely important and profoundly disturbing book'
ARCHBISHOP DESMOND TUTU

The Story of a Political Murder and an African Regime Gone Bad

MICHELA WRONG

'A withering assault on the murderous regime of Kagame, and a melancholy love song to the last dreams of the African Great Lakes'
JOHN LE CARRÉ

SPECIAL REPORT

"These days, oppressed people channel all their
political frustrations via the green movement"

A PROTESTER IN ISTANBUL DURING THE ENVIRONMENTAL PROTEST KNOWN AS 'OCCUPY GEZI' | IT'S NOT EASY BEING GREEN P46

It's not easy being green

KAYA GENÇ finds that environmental activism is alive and well in Turkey, despite the peddling of conspiracy theories and government efforts to discredit campaigners

"FUNDED BY GEORGE Soros and the Rockefeller family, Greenpeace organises chaotic events around the world, spearheading protest movements against the construction of the Istanbul Canal," Yeni Akit, the Turkish government's favourite far-right newspaper, reported recently.

The artificial sea-level waterway,

if it gets built, will connect Marmara with the Black Sea, with an outcome most experts agree will be catastrophic for Istanbul and the Marmara Sea. But Turkey's Islamist government brands anyone opposing its ecocidal project as traitors and foreign agents.

"Greenpeace issued a statement, 'No to the Istanbul Canal', on its website,

insistently disseminating the lie that this project will harm the environment," the pro-government daily warned, calling the canal "the project of the century" and describing criticisms and warnings from activists, experts and scientists as "mere propaganda".

Attacks on environmental activists have never been greater in Turkey, where

ABOVE: Firefighters tackle a blaze in Milas, Mugla, Turkey on 7 August.

laws passed under the state of emergency in 2016 continue to allow Islamists to detain dissidents and NGO workers as "terrorist sympathisers".

For Özgür Gürbüz, one of Turkey's most seasoned environmental activists, the atmosphere of 2021 is reminiscent of the early 2000s.

Since the 1990s, Gürbüz has organised petitions against the construction of nuclear plants in Turkey; marched outside embassies to protest against nuclear projects by

Chinese, French, Japanese and Russian companies; and once walked, backwards, from Mersin to Akkuyu – a 170km journey – to make his voice heard.

One of Turkey's first environmental reporters, Gürbüz worked for the liberal Yeni Yüzyıl newspaper in 1996 when he began covering protests against Turkey's first gold mine in the Anatolian town of Bergama. The Canadian company that operated the mine used cyanide in the extraction process. Villagers who opposed the technique placed ballot boxes in Bergama's town square and held a vote, using direct democracy to settle the issue. They also travelled to Istanbul and, wearing Asterix and Obelix costumes, walked on the city's Bosphorus Bridge carrying banners that read: "Hey police, first listen to what we have to say, then you can beat us!"

Gürbüz frequently travelled from Istanbul to Bergama to cover the protests. "Then one day," he recalled, "a massive conspiracy theory, designed to demonise Bergama's villagers, emerged."

According to the ultra-nationalist press, tales about cyanide were but a plot devised by a network of German NGOs, spearheaded by the Heinrich Böll Foundation, to bring Turkey to its knees. Ankara's State Security Court opened a case in 2002, where 15 NGO workers faced spying charges which carried prison sentences of up to 15 years.

Meanwhile, a Turkish mining company called Koza had taken control of Bergama's mine. Gürbüz smelt a rat. Whenever he called Koza, the company's press officer asked him: "Do you know what German NGOs had been doing here? Let me send you a cache of information!" But a brief glimpse at the documents showed they contained nothing "but unfounded claims".

Gürbüz believes Koza had disseminated disinformation to dissuade patriotic Turks who supported the uprising from opposing their takeover. It later transpired that Koza was one of the companies operated by the movement of Fetullah Gülen, the Islamist preacher

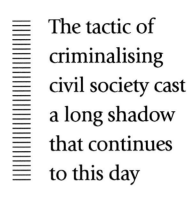

The tactic of criminalising civil society cast a long shadow that continues to this day

who allied with president Recep Tayyip Erdoğan in the 2000s to purge secularists from Turkey's public sector.

This tactic of criminalising civil society cast a long shadow that continues to this day.

"Sometimes they accuse us of being German spies; other times we're British collaborators. Countries change; the accusation of being in the pay of foreign powers does not," Gürbüz said. "But their accusations devastated Bergama villagers. I know them. They love their soil, and all they wanted was to practice agriculture.

"They are patriots, typical Anatolian people who suddenly found themselves on the telly, portrayed as German and British agents. It was impossible for them not to panic."

For scholars and experts who worked for environmental causes, the prospect of a knock on the door from the security services became a real possibility. "The public broadcaster TRT gave airtime to the disinformation campaign featuring German NGOs. Such speculation exhausted and harmed Turkey's burgeoning environmental movement," said Gürbüz.

The spying case that began in 2002 came to nothing. Still, its mentality set the tone for the oppression of green activists over the next two decades, casting doubts on international NGOs just as the climate crisis worsened.

"Those who environmentalists rattle use whatever tool that comes in handy for them," Gürbüz said, pointing to Aysin and Ali Ulvi Büyüknohutçu, a →

→ couple in their 60s known for their environmental activism in south-west Turkey, who were murdered in 2017. Gürbüz said: "They were trying to defend their environment. They received no funding, and yet the forces opposed to their struggle hired a young man to shoot them with a hunting rifle."

Gürbüz sees a pattern in these cases where polluters use Turkey's xenophobic climate to blame NGOs that oppose their ecocidal projects.

"Other tactics include tax controls, sending inspectors to NGOs to intimidate their workers," he said.

To counter such manoeuvres, Gürbüz believes, journalists must act boldly. "In the past, we used to deal directly with the government because most polluters were public bodies. With the new autocratic regime, things are different. Private company CEOs are friends of newspaper tycoons who have ties to the government. Thanks to these intricate ties, the field for environmental journalism has shrunk."

Gürbüz has suffered numerous instances of censorship. After identifying heavy metals in fish samples from the Marmara Sea, his newspaper refused to print the word "tuna" to avoid angering advertisers. (He published the uncensored version on his blog.) When he travelled to Yatağan to report on the public health implications of a thermic plant, his editor refused to publish the report, fearing that the company behind the project might become the newspaper's new owner.

"This is why independent media is so crucial for the environmental struggle," Gürbüz said.

After his reporting career came to an end, he spent a year in China before, on returning to Turkey, entering the NGO world, working for Greenpeace Mediterranean's energy campaign and moving to the Heinrich Böll Foundation to become project co-ordinator, overseeing which projects to fund. He also worked for WWF Turkey.

Then, in 2013, everything changed with Occupy Gezi, the biggest environmentalist protest in Turkey's history.

"Thousands of people marched there, and they managed to save the park," he said. "Honestly, it isn't easy to see how such events begin and shapeshift. A handful of my friends who were collecting signatures outside Gezi suddenly saw their supporters snowball into thousands after bulldozers entered the park and cops burned their tents."

As Gezi grew, Turkey's Islamists once again branded environmental activists as foreign agents funded by "the interest lobby", a dog-whistle term used to appeal to their antisemitic voters. Pro-government papers identified the German airline company Lufthansa's jealousy of Istanbul's planned new airport as the reason behind "the German hand" in protests.

But Gürbüz said: "If you want the

BELOW: People gather to protest the Canal Istanbul project which will link the seas north and south of the city

agents behind Gezi, why don't you look at the people who advised the government to build a shopping mall there in the first place? If it weren't for them, these protests would never have happened."

And yet their rabid discourse is still with us. Dozens of scientists, environmentalists and scholars have written extensively about the Istanbul Canal's disastrous effects, and "it would be a strategic mistake for the government to try to present this as another foreign-funded opposition campaign", Gürbüz said – but that is precisely what is happening. "This discourse is an insult to the mind of this nation."

In 2008, Gürbüz served as a co-founder of Yeşiller (Green Party), the second iteration of a party that originally launched in 1988. The original Yeşiller emerged as a fresh voice in the leftist circles that the 12 September coup in 1980 destroyed.

Koray Doğan Urbarlı, a green activist, has childhood memories of Yeşiller's early protests. He said: "In 1990, when I was five, Yeşiller held a meeting in Izmir to oppose the construction of the Aliağa Thermal Power Plant. My parents also brought me to the Yatağan protests. I later learned that those were all Yeşiller events."

In August 2008, Urbarlı attended a meeting organised by Yeşiller. The party was a month old, and it changed his life. Helping found its local Izmir branches, he devoted his life to Yeşiller.

There he also met Emine Özkan. Born in 1993, Özkan had spent her youth in an ultra-conservative family in Eskişehir, specialising in bird migration before starting work for NGOs. Today, Urbarlı and Özkan are spokespeople for Yeşiller's third iteration.

"There was a straight line between bird preservation and politics," Özkan said. "I discovered how LGBT rights, children's rights and disability activism are all connected. Yet, as individuals, there is a limit to what we can achieve. The more we can organise this into a political struggle, the more we can deliver change."

 ## His editor refused to publish the report, fearing that the company behind the project might become the newspaper's new owner

When she first entered the green struggle, just a few activists in Turkey were aware of the impending climate crisis. "Now, it impacts our lives daily. It adds to other problems: Turkey's autocratic regime and economic crisis. What we have known and said in the background for years is now coming to the fore," she said, adding that as authoritarianism increases and trust in the government diminishes, environmental NGOs and the women's movement are on the rise.

"These days, oppressed people channel all their political frustrations via the green movement," said Urbarlı, who accepts that talking critically about ecological issues is easier than in other fields in Turkey, such as those of minority or LGBT rights.

"In the past, we were seen as marginal figures; now what we say plays a crucial part in political debates."

It's little wonder Yeşiller is receiving the government's cold shoulder. Despite submitting all the required documents on 21 September 2020, it has received no word from the Interior Ministry, which refuses to acknowledge it as a political party. "They neither deny nor affirm us. This violates our civil rights," the co-founders said.

Turkey's constitution clarifies that no one has the power to prevent a party's foundation, and yet the government has "placed Yeşiller in limbo".

Despite state muzzling, Yeşiller is hopeful for the future. "Looking at Occupy Gezi eight years on, we can see that the principles we held dear during the foundation of Yeşiller in 2008 were realised in the form of peaceful resistance, with demands for local democracy and gender equality," Urbarlı said. "Gezi helped disseminate green

ideas to bigger crowds, and it enlightens our ideas to this day."

But the government's xenophobic discourse has proved to be similarly resistant. When wildfires broke out in the country's forests in late July, a social media campaign targeted Yeşiller after the party's Twitter account pointed to climate change as the cause of the fires.

Pro-government newspapers said "Kurdish terrorists" were behind the fires; one journalist blamed the planting of "traitorous" pine trees as part of the Marshall Plan in the 1950s, calling it a sinister plan devised by "US imperialism" to burn Turkey to the ground with help from its "traitorous" local collaborators. The post was shared and liked by thousands.

"These conspiracy theories make people feel safe," Özkan said. "This is the difficulty of environmental politics today. Despite these lynching attempts, we have to continue telling the truth."

Urbarlı envisages a future in which the party can serve in a coalition government, anticipated to be formed after the general elections that are scheduled for 2023.

"It's easy to be an environmentalist when you're in the opposition," he said, highlighting the example of Erdoğan, the Istanbul Canal's architect, who used to conduct press conferences with Yeşiller to defend freedom of expression decades ago when he was the Istanbul head of the Islamist Welfare Party.

"Such is the difference between being in opposition and power, and it is a lesson we should learn from." ✖

Kaya Genç is a contributing editor to Index on Censorship. He lives in Istanbul

50(03):46/49|DOI:10.1177/03064220211048860

It's in our nature to fight

BETH PITTS hears how Ecuador's indigenous people are campaigning to safeguard their history and secure their future

ECUADOR IS NOT a safe country for environmental defenders. They are criminalised, threatened, attacked and even assassinated for attempting to uphold the rights of nature decreed in the constitution.

While the overt incitement to hatred against environmental activists ended when Lenin Moreno replaced Rafael Correa as president in 2017, and some imprisoned indigenous leaders were freed, the intimidation and threats continue.

In 2018, there were several attacks against members of the Collective of Amazonian Women who work to

defend the Amazon region from oil and mining. Margoth Escobar had her house set on fire and Patricia Gualinga, from Sarayaku, had rocks thrown through her bedroom windows at night. Others received death threats.

The same year, three water defenders – including Yaku Pérez Guartambel, then president of indigenous peoples' organisation Ecuarunari – were kidnapped by mine workers, believed to have been following orders from above. An angry mob kicked, dragged and tortured Pérez Guartambel, accusing him of leading anti-mining efforts. They

planned on crucifying him and started gathering materials until a group of journalists broke through with cameras and rescued him.

Since a 2019 uprising of indigenous peoples in the country, the government has more forcefully set its sights on the indigenous movement as the internal enemy to be defeated.

Indigenous leaders are repeatedly persecuted and intimidated. The repressive apparatus has been strengthened, with millions of dollars allocated for the provision of equipment for the police and military. The creation

LEFT: The Sarayaku believe they will be a pillar of resistance after other communities have surrendered

We have almost no resources, almost no fish, almost no animals to hunt

of a new legal framework in May 2020 would have enabled the deployment of the military to control internal order. This would have provided protection to strategic sectors such as mining, against which indigenous communities have been struggling for years.

In May 2021, right-wing banker Guillermo Lasso assumed the presidency in Ecuador, ending more than a decade of left-wing rule. Index on Censorship spoke to Franco-Brazilian academic and indigenous rights activist Manuela Picq about what the change means for censorship. After marrying Yaku Pérez Guartambel in an indigenous ceremony, Picq was herself censored by the government of Rafael Correa, which forced her into a three-year exile.

"There are many ways of censoring. We have seen traditional censorship mostly from the left in Ecuador, by Correa in particular, who implemented very repressive media legislation and enforced it with violent oppression. Then there are other forms of censorship, which are not traditionally recognised as such, the neo-liberal way of buying support. Under Lasso, journalists and media outlets are not fulfilling their critical role because they receive so much state advertising revenue. I see this as a form of censorship, when the public is left uninformed about the government's activities, which happen largely in the dark. In this context, whistle blowers will play a critical role," said Picq.

"This is a weak government that has been forced to ally with Pachakutik, the political party of Ecuador's indigenous movement, which is currently presiding over congress. This means Lasso will carry out his agenda in the most discreet way possible, to avoid being overthrown. So, mining in indigenous territories, or the privatisation of the public sector will be labelled as "development". We are

relieved in Ecuador that we no longer have Correa-ism, with its traditional, explicit forms of censorship, but we should not underestimate the other forms of censorship that are more subtle and insidious."

The multicoloured people

Jimmy Piaguaje is a young indigenous Siekopai defender from Siekoya Remolino, a community of 53 families living on the banks of the Aguarico River in the north-eastern Ecuadorian Amazon region.

The Siekopai (which means multicoloured people) are renowned for their shamanic acumen and knowledge of medicinal plants, with uses for more than 1,000 different plants.

In the 1600s, when Jesuit missionaries arrived in Siekopai territory, there were 30,000 to 40,000 Siekopai in the zone between Putumayo, the Aguarico River and Napo.

Traditionally, the Siekopai lived

communally in gigantic *malokas* (open sided wooden huts) with 40 to 60 families. This coexistence meant that people did everything together. Everyone got up at about 3am to prepare and drink *yoko*, twist threads of *chambira* (a palm from which the fibre is removed to make hammocks) and tell stories. The women would discuss what they would do that day, what the future would bring. The children would be there, too, learning from their parents and elders.

The missionaries brought illnesses such as measles, wiping out 90% of the population. Whole peoples and clans disappeared. The few who survived did so by hiding in the depths of the jungle. Then the rubber-tappers arrived and removed the Siekopai from there, too.

Currently only around 1,600 Siekopai remain – 900 in Peru and 700 in Ecuador, where they live in a 50,000-acre fragment of rainforest.

"We feel very threatened, very worried, because our territory is ➔

BELOW: The Siekopai, who live in the north-east of Ecuador, are known as the multicoloured people

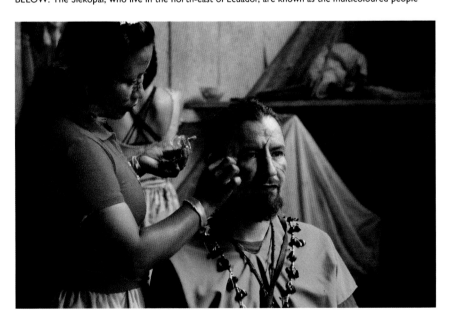

Will our culture survive another five, 10, 20 years? Or will we just die?

→ very small and we are surrounded by oil exploitation and monoculture agriculture," said Piaguaje.

"I know from talking with my father, with our elders, how our territory used to be. Now we have almost no resources, almost no fish, no animals to hunt. Our rivers are contaminated by toxic waste from the oil palm industry. Lack of food sovereignty is a really big worry. These are the threats that we are facing.

"All of these things have made us think about where we are going. Will our culture survive another five, 10, 20 years? Or will we just die?"

The pandemic, too, has had a deep impact on the Siekopai.

"In the Ecuadorian Amazon, the Siekopai nationality was the first to confirm positive cases of Covid-19," said Piaguaje. "A wise elder who died of Covid – a family member of mine – knew a lot

about medicinal plants. That was major blow for the Siekopai because there aren't many of us and we all know each other. Then a teacher died; he had long been involved in the struggle to defend our culture. It was a very difficult situation."

The Siekopai sought help from the local and national governments but there was little or no response, although some organisations provided medicine, tests and accurate information.

"We started to realise that the medicine from outside wasn't helping us," said Piaguaje. "Faced with many cases of Covid, we started to look to medicinal plants. In the end, the majority of people who survived were treated with medicinal plants. And we're still treating people with plant infusions, such as *ajo del monte, chinchona* and *cedros*, with good results.

"This has led to some very important

reflections within the Siekopai communities; a rediscovery, appreciation and faith in our own ancestral medicines. And when everything collapsed in the outside world, although we were affected, we were more or less OK. This has been a deep reflection for us, seeing how the rest of the world is suffering and realising what is important."

In response to the existential threats they face, Piaguaje and a group of other young Siekopai leaders have formed an organisation, Sëra, named after the spirit of heaven that arrives every summer to announce a new era. They have developed a number of innovative projects, safeguarding ancestral shamanic knowledge in video format and running environmental workshops with Siekopai youth.

"Ancestral knowledge is being rapidly lost," he said. "Young people are no longer interested, due to the influence of the Western world. Our wise elders are

BELOW: Just 1,600 Siekopai survive in a 50,000-acre fragment of rainforest

dying without leaving a legacy.

"Together with another young Siekopai defender, I created a project to safeguard their knowledge with videos. We go out with them when they are harvesting plants and record them talking about how they identify and use them. This project brought our group of young leaders together."

The group is now running school workshops to promote environmental awareness through intergenerational exchange between elders, parents and children.

"We talk about ancestral knowledge, the identification and uses of medicinal plants, the threats that we face. We ask, what is important to us, what do we want to preserve, as Siekopai? The aim is to instil in the children the consciousness that our territory matters, that they should have respect for the elders, for Mother Nature, for our own cosmovision [the worldviews shared by indigenous peoples].

"We know that the children are like seeds; if we plant in them the idea that they must cut down the jungle to plant oil palm, they will want to do that," he said.

"But instead we are saying to them, 'We must take care of the jungle, this is our wealth, there are other ways to do things, to survive'. That's why I think education is so important."

Piaguaje believes it can help combat climate change.

"The indigenous worldview is based on living in harmony with nature and other people, respecting everything around us," he said.

"It is a model that does not require us to plunder all natural resources. We are taught that we are all part of Mother Nature, that it is our responsibility to use resources in a sustainable way.

"Mother Nature provides everything: medicine, food, water and air. We don't need to destroy but to co-exist.

"This way of life is based on reciprocity. Even if the other person is different from me, we share. Sharing and co-operation. That is how our ancestors lived and that should be the model of how we live, too.

"I think a global shift towards these values could help to combat climate change."

The People of Noon

José Gualinga is a leader of the Native People of Sarayaku, an indigenous Kichwa group with 1,400 inhabitants living in a remote part of Ecuador's southern Amazon.

Known for their defence of the rights of nature and indigenous peoples, the Sarayaku call themselves the People of Noon, referring to an ancient prophecy of their ancestors claiming that they would be a pillar of resistance after other communities had surrendered – a beacon of light as strong as the midday sun.

In 2012, the Sarayaku won a historic victory at the Inter-American Court of Human Rights, which found that the Ecuadorian state had violated their rights by allowing an oil company to prospect in their territory without consultation.

A turning point in the case came when José's father, Don Sabino Gualinga, the spiritual leader of Sarayaku and their most eminent yachak (shaman), then aged 92, took the witness stand. He was asked about the impact of the 1,433kg of explosives that had been planted in Sarayaku territory by the oil company, accompanied by armed military personnel. Referring to the invisible beings that had been disturbed by the explosions, Don Sabino said that "half of the masters of the jungle are no longer there".

He added: "It is a living forest. There are trees and medicinal plants and all kinds of beings … Many hid, others died when it burst. They are the ones who maintain the jungle, the forest … All of those who wish to cause damage, they don't understand what they are doing. We do understand it, because we see it."

The same year, the Sarayaku created the Kawsak Sacha (Living Forest) Declaration asserting that, as a living entity, their territory is subject to legal rights and demanding that these rights be upheld. The proposal was presented at global climate change conference COP21 in Paris and to French president François Hollande in 2015, and to the Ecuadorian government in 2018 before winning the prestigious UN Equator Prize in 2021. The Sarayaku have also launched a professional football team to spread the word about oil exploitation in the Amazon; sailed a canoe down the Seine; and created a documentary, Children of the Jaguar, which won best documentary at the National Geographic Film Festival in 2012. Their 2021 documentary, The Return, which tells the story of one family's retreat into the Amazon to escape Covid, was made for The Guardian and featured at the 2021 Sheffield DocFest.

In 2021, the Sarayaku are once again under threat, with the government's plan to auction three million hectares of largely virgin rainforest to oil companies, including nearly all the Sarayaku territory. To represent their peaceful resistance to extractivism and commitment to defend the Kawsak Sacha, the Sarayaku are planting a 100km-long perimeter of flowering trees around their territory known as the Sisa Ñampi; it symbolises the fragility of life and the ephemeral limit of existence between life and death.   →

We believe that if the human being accepts this way of life, the pain of the planetary wound will be felt, healed, and life will be born again

Gualinga believes that the philosophical thought of the Sarayaku can help combat climate change.

"Climate change will be resolved only if we actively seek solutions," he said. "Global citizens must undertake a long road to resistance and peaceful struggle, towards a different perspective that we call *tiam*. By itself this philosophical thought is only a form of knowledge, but it can be made reality if each and every one of us participates in the *minga* [collective community work].

"*Tiam* is a counterpoint to the dominant worldview, which sees nature as 'other', as an object for exploitation. This has led to imbalance and severe climatic changes, as well as the current pandemic. At the heart of our philosophy lies the understanding that we live as an embryo in the womb of the Pachamama [Mother Earth]. Only in this way will nature be respected, will we live harmoniously, benefiting from the resources that the Pachamama bestows on us.

"We believe that if the human being accepts this way of life, the pain of the planetary wound will be felt, healed, and life will be born again."

He added: "Indigenous peoples are already contributing towards global climate change solutions by taking care of their territories, which are mega-diversities of living beings. The Sarayaku conceived the Kawsak Sacha life project as a powerful nucleus, so that through these invisible beings, who are conscious and therefore have legal rights, we can regulate the balance of the earth and together we can fight climate change."

Many communities of indigenous peoples have been divided by oil companies but the Sarayaku have maintained unity, said Gualinga.

"The unity of the Sarayaku arises from the legacy of our ancestors, from

ABOVE: Siekopai community life continues despite the arrival of Covid-19

the great stories and prophecies that have led us to consider ourselves as the People of Noon, descendants of the jaguar, children of Amazanga Runa," he said.

"Other nationalities – let us call them 'communities' or 'peoples' – their unity is maintained in a superficial way, through an organisation. While the statute of the organisation may be recognised by the competent authorities, the people lack the background of using their history and wisdom as a strength.

"When the unity of a society – or let's call it a 'cultural civilisation' – of the Amazon forest is founded on historical and cultural principle, the oil companies cannot break it."

The people of Sarayaku are masters in the selective use of modern technology, such as digital resource mapping, and using social networks without losing their cultural identity.

"If well used, technology can serve to strengthen new processes of collective and organised adaptation," said Gualinga. "Based on this logic and analysis, the people of Sarayaku have adopted certain tools, such as the internet, which we use to disseminate

the processes resistance in defence of our lives; to make known the proposals that come from within the territory and from the deep jungle. The jungle society has always been in a state of interaction, actively looking for solutions for threats such as climate change.

"Historically, it was impossible to make visible Sarayaku's proposals in a dominant, complex world, full of wars and devastating economic conflicts. Now, with these new technologies, we can successfully disseminate communications on history, culture, proposals, visionary projects to conserve and protect the balance of the land and ensure the continuity of the Living Forest.

"These technologies have also allowed us to safeguard the memories of art, culture and stories, so that future generations can continue learning." ✖

Help the Siekopai Indigenous Amazonian Youth Foundation through its crowdfunding campaign at gofundme.com/f/siekopai-indigenous-amazonian-youth-foundation.

This article is based on interviews for Writers Rebel (writersrebel.com)

Beth Pitts *is the author of the Moon guide to Ecuador & the Galápagos Islands (2019), which focuses on ethical travel. She has worked with indigenous Ecuadorean communities since 2013.*

We live as an embryo in the womb on Mother Earth

50(03):50/54|DOI:10.1177/03064220211048861

Respect for tradition

Australia has a history of "selective listening" when it comes to First Nations voices. Now Yvonne Weldon is aiming to become the first Aboriginal Lord Mayor of Sydney, reports **EMILY BROWN**

ABOVE: Aboriginal hunters in Manyallaluk

THE BUSHFIRES THAT tore across Australia in the summer of 2019-20 left in their wake 18 million hectares of scorched land. A total of 33 people – including nine firefighters – lost their lives, and close to 3,500 homes were razed to the ground. Ecologists calculated that as many as one billion animals perished in the fires, while economists estimated the cost of recovery at an unprecedented AU$100 billion.

Faced with tallies of destruction too big to comprehend, Australians cast about for clarity on why this disaster was unfolding, and how it could be prevented from happening again the future. Conveniently, there was a living culture with 65,000 years of experience in caring for the country to turn to for answers.

The fires precipitated a sudden torrent of interest in traditional Aboriginal land management techniques. First Nations rangers, practitioners and traditional knowledge experts – so rarely afforded time on the airwaves – were widely consulted on national television and radio shows. For many Australians, it was their first time hearing about "cool burning" and "fire-stick farming": traditional methods of burning patches of bushland at low temperatures to clear the undergrowth without damaging root systems and curtail the risk of out-of-control bushfires in the arid heights of summer.

Yet these practices are ancient. They've been passed down through ➔

Aboriginal people are not one people – there are hundreds of different nations and tribes and clans all across the country

→ generations of Aboriginal Australians, forming part of the symbiotic relationship that First Nations people have with the environment as custodians of the land.

"Think of it like this: an Aboriginal man 300 years ago didn't have to worry about handing a climate emergency on to the next generation," said indigenous cultural educator and Wiradjuri man Darren Charlwood.

"What they were handing on to their children was an understanding of how to survive, how to respect their country, how to respect their ancestors in doing so, and how to practise all this through land management, through ritual, through their interactions within their social organisation and systems."

While the unprecedented interest in traditional knowledge from the media, the government and conservation organisations was undeniably welcome, for educators such as Charlwood – who works for Sydney's Royal Botanical Gardens and the New South Wales government's National Parks and Wildlife Service – it was also frustrating.

"If that sort of engagement had come into play a lot earlier, we probably wouldn't have had as big a catastrophe as we did," he said. "Traditional fire management is wonderful, and it can really help with the plight of our environment in Australia. But, mind you, this was a climate catastrophe. Traditional land management would have saved only so much. The bottom line is the climate is changing."

The consultation-after-the-fact that occurred in the wake of the 2019-20 bushfires is symptomatic of a more troubling "selective listening" that Australia's First Nations people encounter across the political spectrum

– from the prime minister's office to the halls of local government – especially on land and environment issues. It's something that Yvonne Weldon, Australia's first Aboriginal candidate for Lord Mayor of Sydney, is looking to change.

For Weldon, the principle of inclusion is at the core of an indigenous approach to leadership and environmentalism. It's a value she places at the heart of her campaign.

"Inclusion is who we are as First Nations people," she said. "Our ability to be inclusive – to hear what others are saying and act with sensitivity to their existence – is how we have been able to survive."

She added that the same logic applied to the environment. "Prior to Invasion we didn't have polluted parts of our country. We didn't take any more than was needed. Whatever ecosystem you were a part of, you had to live in harmony with it. You didn't do it at the expense of other living things."

Reaching for the top

Weldon and her team at Unite for Sydney launched their campaign at Redfern Oval in May, nearly 20 years after then-prime minister Paul Keating's historic Redfern Speech, where he recognised the impact of dispossession and oppression on First Nations peoples, and called for their place in the modern Australian nation to be cemented.

"It's about creating moments that represent a landmark for inclusion," explained Weldon. "And, hopefully, those moments happen closer and closer together in time until inclusion is no longer the exception, it's commonplace."

Weldon is a proud Wiradjuri woman who grew up in the inner-city suburb

of Redfern, Sydney. With 30 years of experience as a community organiser and campaigner, she has spent her adult life advocating for the disadvantaged. She is a board member of Domestic Violence NSW and Redfern Jarjum College – a primary school supporting Aboriginal and Torres Strait Islander children needing additional learning support – as well as deputy chair of the NSW Australia Day Council. She's also the first Aboriginal person to run for the top job at the City of Sydney Council.

"To me, the fact that I'm the first Aboriginal person to run for Lord Mayor of Sydney in 2021 is insulting," she said. "It's an insult because it hasn't been done before in this country, and yet we think we have progressed."

Running on a platform of effective climate action, genuinely affordable housing and better community engagement, the campaigner-turned-candidate sees plenty of opportunities for improvement.

"True leadership has to be inclusive of all, and what I've seen in local government has fallen way short of that."

She realised she had to take a run at the job after six years as elected chair of Sydney's Metropolitan Local Aboriginal Land Council (LALC) – an organisation set up by law to advocate for the interests of local Aboriginal people in relation to land acquisition, use and management.

In her experience, representatives of the City of Sydney Council have chosen to engage only when it suits their purposes, and either reject proposals for meaningful change out of hand or use inordinate process as a way of keeping them in check.

It's an all-too-familiar story in Australia, where the government has been unwilling to reach a treaty with its indigenous people comparable to those of New Zealand, Canada or the USA.

Aboriginal calls for recognition were formalised in 2017 with the Uluru Statement from the Heart, which called for a First Nations Voice enshrined in the constitution, and a treaty to supervise agreement-making and truth-telling with governments.

But the historical consensus was rejected outright by then-prime minister Malcolm Turnbull and denigrated by the deputy prime minister, Barnaby Joyce, who called it an "overreach".

Following a 2018 parliamentary inquiry which found the Statement from the Heart should indeed be enacted, the current Australian government has delayed plans to introduce relevant legislation until after the next federal election in 2022.

A long fight

The application of "selective listening" to First Nations calls for autonomy over their own land is, historically speaking, one of the foundations that modern Australia was built on.

"The damage that's been done to Australia over 250 years of not respecting indigenous people or knowledge… you can really see it in our environment, it's very much on show," said Charlwood. "Because of the way that people have introduced invasive animals and plants to Australia, because of practices like mining and the way people engage with the landscape here, Australia has lost more wildlife in a shorter time than anywhere else on Earth."

According to Heather Goodall – professor emerita of history at the University of Technology in Sydney – there is historical evidence that Aboriginal people in New South Wales made efforts to secure broad tracts of land where they could feel a sense of safety and belonging, access sites of cultural significance and act as custodians for the environment as early as the 1840s, when the first "reserves" were established.

ABOVE: Lord Mayor of Sydney's first aboriginal candidate Yvonne Weldon. Picture in January 2019 on Australia Day.

Despite a movement which involved direct action, writing their own petitions and recruiting sympathetic white men to convey their demands to authorities, Aboriginal people were gradually moved to government-delineated reserves, missions or small parcels of land for agricultural use.

"Consultation is often about seeking opinions which will be used to justify a decision that has already been made. It's a very hard-to-define term that often doesn't mean having decision-making power," said Goodall.

That's a sentiment Weldon can relate to. "Aboriginal people are not one people – there are hundreds of different nations and tribes and clans all across the country," she said.

"Bearing in mind the diversity of Aboriginal Australia, often what people in power do is if they don't want to hear what one group has to say, they'll go to another group until they find someone to say what they want to hear. I call it 'shopping around'.

"They'll play people off each other, they'll offer little crumbs, they'll do all these types of things because that's the colonial viewpoint. It's about creating the notion that you're open and inclusive, when actually you're orchestrating it all for self.

"Sydney represents ground zero, where the impact of colonisation began," she added. "But you can't talk about reviving or respecting traditional knowledge if you're not inclusive of First Nations people."

As another generation of Aboriginal Australians stands ready to share knowledge and lead the way to a more sustainable future, the question remains whether other Australians are ready to listen – and ready to vote. ✖

Emily Brown is a Sydney-based writer and editor covering art, cities, and social justice

50(03):55/57|DOI:10.1177/03064220211048863

 The fires precipitated a sudden torrent of interest in traditional Aboriginal land management techniques

The write way to fight

ABOVE: A protest against BP at the National Portrait Gallery in London

LIZ JENSEN explains how a group of writers joined forces to build a literary response to the climate crisis

WHEN WRITERS REBEL (WR) formed to become Extinction Rebellion's (XR's) literary wing in the summer of 2019, our aim was to put literature in the service of the threatened ecosystems that sustain us.

One of our inspirations was the Indian novelist Amitav Ghosh's 2016 book, The Great Derangement, which criticised literary fiction's failure to address climate and ecological breakdown.

"It's our job, as writers, to make imaginative leaps on behalf of those who don't, can't or won't," he wrote.

His book unsettled me. He was right that most fiction wasn't rising to the occasion, but I wanted him to be wrong.

Then, in the early summer of 2019, I spotted a tweet by novelist Monique Roffey asking if there were any other writers concerned about the climate and the ecological emergency. I responded – and so did the novelist and academic James Miller. Our initial conversations revolved around how to engage our creative writing students and fellow writers on the biggest issue of our times. But our good intentions felt tame, so I called my younger son.

The previous year, at the age of 23, Raphaël Coleman had joined XR and found his tribe.

Raphaël – who played the role of Colin Firth's unruly boffin son, Eric Brown, in the 2005 film Nanny McPhee – was an early recruit to XR's media and messaging team. Known in XR as Iggy Fox, Raphaël was active in XR Youth and he introduced us to screenwriter Jessica Townsend. Before we knew it, we were working within XR.

Monique, Jessica, James and I were soon joined by the Mexican novelist Chloe Aridjis, and by the time we had decided on a name our core group had expanded to half a dozen. We knew that if we could assemble enough writers we could be part of the upcoming October Rebellion, so we hit our contacts lists.

Soon, Naomi Alderman, Susie Orbach, Philip Hoare, AL Kennedy, Romesh Gunesekera and Ali Smith had signed up. Some of Britain's top literary figures agreed to perform, unpaid, from a soapbox on an illegally held site. When

Margaret Atwood sent us her blessings and agreed to appear on XR's podcast with Jessica, we felt another shift. By now we had 40 writers for our three-hour event – and a waiting list.

The rebellion began. I met Raphaël the day before our event in a café on Charing Cross Road. He was evading the police. He sat on his phone, and advised me to do the same, as he told me in a low voice some of what he'd been up to – including running the team claiming Trafalgar Square, where we'd been promised a platform. Now we were not just mother and son but fellow rebels.

What we came to call The Marathon was a high-risk undertaking: a far cry from Cheltenham or Hay-on-Wye, and like no literary festival any of us had been involved in before. The crazy literary extravaganza included bravura performances from AL Kennedy, Salena Godden, David Graeber, Irenosen Okojie, M John Harrison, Simon Schama and dozens more.

Hundreds of people crowded onto the pavement to watch. The sun shone, and the police looked on, bemused. When it started to pour, we decamped to the shelter of an archway next to Waterstones, and the show went on.

Soon after, one of our most stirring performers, novelist Toby Litt, joined the core team, and the American novelist Jenny Offill contacted us asking how she could help. "Set up WR in New York," we replied. And before we knew it, she, Elissa Schappell, Nick Laird and other writers had done just that.

By the new year, Toby, James and our new team member Beth Pitts, a freelance activist-journalist based in Ecuador (see her article on page 50), were building our website, commissioning blogs and scheduling the weekly newsletters which are central to our output.

The site's launch, paired with the social media following built up by James,

....

RIGHT: Author Zadie Smith speaks at an XR Writers Rebel event in London

Nobody is gagging us, but the struggle is for a space to be heard

was a step-change for our group, and added excitement to our weekly Zooms.

As a small team of us began working on a Rebel Library as a resource for the site, Raphaël was expanding the wildlife workers' network, The Wildwork, he founded as a student, and planning a documentary film about the all-female anti-poaching squads in South Africa and Zimbabwe. Everything felt like it was moving forward.

Then, shortly after his arrival in South Africa, Raphaël's father phoned me unexpectedly.

Our son was dead.

He'd been running, and he'd collapsed. Later it emerged that his heart had failed due to a previously undiagnosed condition.

"I can't even imagine what it must be like," friends said when they heard the shocking news.

My honest answer, at the time, was "I can't either", because my imagination had failed. Even though I saw his corpse in the South African morgue and touched his cold, lifeless hand, I couldn't imagine him dead. Until then, my biggest fear was that he'd be jailed for vandalising the Brazilian embassy in London some months before.

While we cremated him in South Africa, my colleagues at Writers Rebel joined hundreds of activists attending the vigil XR held in his memory in central London. They remained a vital connection to my sanity in the terrible months that followed. So did the knowledge that part of my healing would lie in honouring Raphaël's spirit in every way I could.

In the blurred time that followed his death I read the blogs we published weekly on our site, such as Homero Aridjis's scathing attack on a forest-despoiling tourist train line through Mexico and powerful addresses to juries by Jay Griffiths and Tom Bullough – part of a rich literary archive of defence statements that had been building since XR began. Their words gave me strength.

As more and more writers from around the world offered us their work, I came to feel that our little group had created something diverse, vibrant, committed and essential.

I wasn't up to planning or participating in Writers Rebel's next major event, which took place in October 2020, in collaboration with XR's Money Rebellion. But the others were there in force, and it was another landmark →

The literary world is waking up to the crisis now yesterday's direst predictions have come true

→ moment. The protest readings were held in Tufton Street, in central London, home of fossil fuel lobbyists and denialist think-tanks. Zadie Smith, George Monbiot, Juliet Stephenson, Mark Rylance, Caroline Lucas and others gave hard-hitting speeches.

WR's Jessica spray-painted the word "Lies" on one of the pillars of the building's façade, and was arrested alongside Prof Rupert Read and XR founder Clare Farrell. They are due to appear in court on 28 October, charged with criminal damage. (You can support the Tufton Three at https://uk.gofundme.com/f/support-the-tufton-3)

A month later, to mark Lost Species Day, Chloe Aridjis, Kelly Hill, Paul Ewen and Alex Lockwood masterminded On the Brink, a huge international Zoom event highlighting endangered wildlife, featuring Margaret Atwood, Ben Okri, Lydia Millet, Amitav Ghosh and other stellar writers championing species threatened with extinction.

This year, On the Brink 2: Insectageddon focused on the crash of the insect population. Meanwhile,

ABOVE: Raphaël Coleman at an XR protest at the Brazilian Embassy in London in August 2019

WR's Amber Massey-Blomfield, Tamzin Pinkerton and Gully Niu have built a taskforce to work on a campaign to persuade the publishing industry to switch to 100% recycled paper.

We also decided to offer a service to our readers and the public in the form of online writing workshops with an ecological focus. The first of these, The Word For World Is Forest, featured masterclasses from Toby Litt, Charlotte du Cann, Laline Paull and the poet Dom Bury. Alongside it, we began publishing instalments of Toby's incisive and essential primer, How To Write A Novel To Save The World.

In late June, to the surprise of Londoners, a huge green and yellow banner appeared on the River Thames, adorned with a two-line poem by Ben Okri grown in living grass by the artist-activists Heather Ackroyd and Dan Harvey. It marked the launch of our Paint the Land campaign, in which much-loved writers and prominent artists teamed up to create messages urging the delegates to the UN's COP26 climate change summit to take action.

The creative team – Kelly Hill, Paul Ewen and I – hope the idea will take root elsewhere and become part of a grassroots global tapestry of geoglyphs.

A third On the Brink event focusing on ocean wildlife is scheduled for October, and our Rebel Library has just launched new monthly themed book lists, curated by librarian Matt Rose.

What has changed since WR began?

Although we can't take the credit for it, there's no doubt that the literary world is waking up to the crisis now that so many of yesterday's dire scientific predictions have come measurably true. Fiction and the public imagination have always fed off one another – perhaps

never more so than now.

At WR, we hope to be both a catalyst and a channel for that evolution.

But those in power are slow to shift their thinking – or refuse to shift it at all.

Today's climate censorship is a shapeshifter. Yesterday's denialists are today's green-washers and purveyors of delayism. Nobody is gagging us, but with so many toxic truths dominating the public conversation, the struggle is for a space to be heard.

In July, almost 18 months after his death, the jury trial of four of Raphaël's fellow activists was presided over by Judge Perrins in Southwark Crown Court – the same judge whose advice was ignored by a jury the previous month when they acquitted seven XR rebels for vandalising the Shell HQ.

Humiliated by the Shell Seven, the judge's advice to the Brazilian embassy jury was more specific and stringent. As a result, three of the four who appeared in court were found guilty. A fifth was self-isolating and is still awaiting trial.

The guilty verdict made me think that historians will look back on this era and note its defining paradox: that while the public was increasingly occupied with the dangers ahead, those in power were either in active denial, busy plotting how best to profit from a range of oncoming disasters, indifferent or – at best – doing far too little, far too late.

But those same historians may also note that today's storytellers, inspired by solid science and the evidence of their own eyes, have begun to reclaim the power of the prophets and seers of past ages by resuming their almost forgotten role as the cognitive avant-garde. And that, collectively, we bear a vital message summed up best by what Raphaël planned to say at his trial: "There is no greater cause to stand for on this green earth than the green earth itself." ✖

Liz Jensen is co-founder of XR Writers Rebel (writersrebel.com)

50(03):58/60|DOI:10.1177/03064220211048862

Change in the pipeline?

Despite one high-profile success by indigenous people in the USA, these communities still face an uphill battle when it comes to stopping the construction of pipelines on their land. **BRIDGET BYRNE** reports

MOST AMERICANS DO not need to worry about the oil pipelines that fuel their cars, and most live with their water supplies comfortably distant from any risk of a spill. Yet indigenous communities in the USA cannot count on having clean drinking water because the country's thirst for gas is fed by pipelines that cross their native lands.

Over the past decade, the construction of three such pipelines has been challenged by environmentalists and indigenous communities due to the risk to the environment and the violation of tribal sovereignty. The Dakota Access Pipeline, the Keystone XL Pipeline, and Line 3 each run through reservation land against the express wishes of the tribes the lands belong to.

The Keystone XL pipeline had its permit cancelled in June 2021 by president Joe Biden's administration. Faith Spotted Eagle, a leading activist against the pipeline and a member of the Ihanktonwan Dakota nation, told The Guardian the executive order was "an act of courage and restorative justice by the Biden administration." The pipeline had faced constant protest from environmental and indigenous groups in the 10 years since it had been proposed. The administration's executive order stated that "the United States must be in a position to exercise vigorous climate leadership in order to achieve a significant increase in global climate action and put the world on a sustainable climate pathway." But what is unclear is why this pipeline is different from any others.

In Minnesota, activists and community members are gathering in response to the Line 3 project that puts the water sources

ABOVE: Construction of the Dakota Access Pipeline near New Salem, North Dakota

of three reservations—Leech Lake, Red Lake, and White Earth—at risk from oil spills and cuts through treaty land in violation of tribal sovereignty.

Tania Aubid, an elderly activist who grew up in treaty territory, carried out a 28-day hunger strike to protest the pipeline.

"It's my future grandchildren and great grandchildren coming standing up to the pipeline... What I'm hoping for is to be able to have a healthier ecosystem for us to be able to live in," she told the Stop Line 3 campaign.

Activists are calling for the government to take similar action against this pipeline. Winona LaDuke, an Ojibwe leader and Indigenous rights organiser who was arrested at a Line 3 protest and spent three nights in jail, →

 Today, Standing Rock people live with the pipeline and continue to struggle to be heard by their local government and financial institutions

→ told online magazine Slate: "Biden's acting like he cancelled one pipeline so he gets a gold star. But you don't get a gold star from Mother Earth to let Line 3 go ahead."

She added: "It's brutal up here. I'm watching a very destructive pipeline tearing through the heart of my territory. That's why Joe Biden should care. Because it's wrong."

The pipeline is disrupting the watershed and traditional wild rice habitats.

A Canadian oil pipeline corporation, Enbridge, has proposed the expansion of Line 3, which was responsible for the worst inland oil spill in US history in 1991. The Biden administration, which is backing Trump-era approval for the pipeline, has turned down any requests for comment.

The Justice Department said the 2020 approval "met its … obligations by preparing environmental assessments" and asked the courts to reject any case brought against the project. This month, the Minnesota Supreme Court upheld state regulators' approval of the project, and Enbridge says the pipeline is on track to be completed by the end of the year.

If a year is a long time in politics, five years is almost an eternity.

In 2016, social media images from the protests at the Standing Rock Reservation in North Dakota and South Dakota shocked Americans. A grassroots movement against Energy Transfer Partners Dakota Access Pipeline caught the nation's attention when activists stood against the construction of the pipeline, creating the single largest gathering of Native Americans in 100 years.

Protesters had to withstand police violence, including excessive use of pepper spray, water sprayed from high-pressure hoses, and attacks from police dogs. The pipeline was planned to run from North Dakota's Bakken oil field to southern Illinois, crossing through the Standing Rock Reservation on the border of North Dakota and South

Dakota and beneath their main water source, Lake Oahe.

Standing Rock is the sixth-largest Native American reservation and home to nearly 9,000 members of the Hunkpapa and Sihasapa bands of Lakota Oyate and the Ihunktuwona and Pabaksa bands of the Dakota Oyate. The community and independent experts believed that a potential rupture of the pipeline was a serious threat to the clean water supply. The path of construction cut through historically and religiously significant land. Finally, the pipeline would disrupt the reservation's natural ecosystem.

This pipeline had been rerouted from crossing the Missouri River near Bismarck, North Dakota, a far wealthier, predominantly white community, over concerns about proximity to water sources and wetlands.

Youth and women's groups from Standing Rock and surrounding communities organised a campaign to block the construction of the pipeline, using the hashtag #noDAPL on social media. "Water protectors" encamped around Standing Rock, creating protests that reached the size of a small city, in an attempt to block construction.

It's my future grandchildren and great grandchildren coming standing up to the pipeline...it's to be able to have a healthier ecosystem for us to be able to live in

The Barack Obama administration halted the construction of the pipeline by executive order. However, in January 2017, the Trump administration issued an order allowing its resumption. The pipeline was completed in April 2017.

Ryan Vizzions began his independent photography career with the 2015 Black Lives Matter protests in Atlanta. When he heard about the #noDAPL protests, he saw the similarities with the civil rights movement. A planned four-day trip to cover it turned into a six-month commitment; he went back to Atlanta just long enough to quit his job and put all his belongings into storage so he could stay with the protests and help stop the pipeline. He captured the police violence in photos, but he also documented the camps which were "filled with song and prayer, ceremony and community".

His images of Standing Rock capture the mistreatment of a community that so much of the USA has ignored. After his images of police violence went viral, money poured in from supporters, turning the camps into communities with enough resources to feed and house protesters.

Vizzons said that by winter, PTSD from the police violence was common throughout the camp and as national attention faded and temperatures dropped, people began leaving.

The community in the camp "was a beautiful moment in history", he said, adding that what made Standing Rock different was how their voices reached their audience: "Mainstream media tried to avoid the Standing Rock movement until social media made it impossible. We were the news, not them and they hated it."

Since the arrival of the first Europeans, North America's indigenous people have been forced off their land and have had to watch as it has been urbanised. The further west mainstream settlements expanded, the more the government would push tribes further off their land by breaking treaty promises and committing or allowing grotesque violence against indigenous people.

Through physical force and economic manipulation, the government forced indigenous people onto the country's most desolate lands in what is now the reservation system, and despite promises of tribal sovereignty on reservations, reservations still face exploitation and violation of land rights while lacking the political voice to stop the government or government-backed corporations.

The Standing Rock episode is one of the most notable modern instances of harassment and discrimination against the American indigenous population, but the struggle to be heard has long been part of being an indigenous person in the USA.

Today, Standing Rock people live with the pipeline and continue the struggle to be heard by their local government and financial institutions. The community faces challenges for which it is less easy to rally support on social media, such as struggling to obtain bank loans or teen depression.

Joseph McNeil, Jr grew up in New York but moved back to his family's home in Standing Rock 34 years ago. He has been a tribal council member and today is the general manager of Standing Rock's wind farm organisation. Striving for energy and financial independence, the Standing Rock Renewable Energy Public Power Authority pursues wind power as a solution that is both green and affordable.

As general manager, McNeil and the authority prioritise balancing Standing Rock's energy needs with environmental protection and climate justice, a fundamental belief that makes the existence of the Standing Rock pipeline untenable. The Standing Rock Council is also working to create a credit union to increase economic stability amongst the native people. With their renewable energy sources and a credit union, the goal is to deconstruct the two major ways their community is oppressed.

McNeil said the reservation faced the constant struggle of not having economic

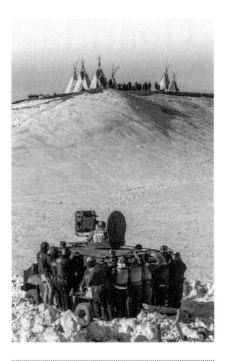

ABOVE: The removal of the last protest camp in Standing Rock, February 2017

assets to pursue their business plans and grow the capital of the reservation. He described the institutional oppression the community faces, saying that "business and government are hand in glove." The reservation system denies land ownership to residents, crippling them economically and politically.

"It's hard to get a home loan if you have an address on the reservation," said McNeil.

He described the psychological impact on his community: "The desperation...the kids didn't have hope... they've seen the cycle of [financial] and emotional poverty"

The lack of opportunity on reservation and the racism they faced off it led to a rash of teen suicides 10 years ago and is a major motivation for the work to provide for the community, who live with the pipeline running through its land.

"I feel devalued when I turn the water on, I feel my kid's lives are devalued," said McNeil. "We fought it tooth and nail. We said no from day one."

Indigenous groups along the Line

3 route are hoping the same does not happen to them.

Earlier this year, activists started creating ceremonial lodges and resistance camps along the path of construction and some attempted to block the work by forming a human chain.

Just like at Standing Rock, the environmental impact report was rushed and incomplete, and police have been using similar aggressive techniques to those seen in 2016 in Standing Rock: rubber bullets, fire hoses, and police attack dogs.

The pipeline is nearing completion, and the three reservations are facing the timeless American practice of exploiting indigenous people's lack voice for the economic gains of mainstream culture.

Stop Line 3 has published its grievances against the pipeline.

Its construction is disrupting shrinking wild rice habitats. Meanwhile, over a 10-year period, according to the US Department of Transportation, an "average" pipeline has a 57% chance of spills.

Stop Line 3 also argues that the state of Minnesota does not have the consent of the tribes or jurisdiction over tribal land and therefore it is a violation of tribal sovereignty and what the organisation calls "modern-day colonialism".

"The phrase 'new oil pipeline' should not even be in our vocabulary," it argues because the overwhelming consensus of scientists is that carbon emissions must be drastically reduced to stop the growing climate crisis.

Once again, indigenous people and big business, and the planet and the government are facing off. That should be food for thought for Americans driving in their gas-guzzlers. ✖

Bridget Byrne is an intern with Index on Censorship through the CAPA network and studies at the University of Maryland, majoring in journalism and government & politics..

50(03):61/63|DOI:10.1177/03064220211048865

The rape of Uganda

The nation's natural resources are being plundered and it's those doing the damage who are being protected, writes **ISSA SIKITI DA SILVA**

UGANDA'S NATURAL RESOURCES base, one of the richest and most diverse in Africa, continues to be degraded, jeopardising both individual livelihoods and the country's economic development.

Evidence from the UN Environment Programme reveals that its forests, home to several endangered or soon-to-be extinct animal and plant species, are being mercilessly ravaged by poachers, illegal charcoal traders and loggers, and greedy investors.

Overfishing in the country's lakes and rivers is rife. Its wetlands are being cleared for agricultural use and the rate of forest cover loss stands at 2.6 per cent annually, according to independent sources.

As part of efforts to ensure that the east African nation's natural resources are effectively managed and protected, a group of environmental activists has gone to war to protect these natural wonders from bleeding further.

"Environmental activism in Uganda is not a safe identity – it's a hostile and fragile environment," William Amanzuru, team leader at Friends of Zoka, told Index.

> ## Perpetrators continue attacking environmental defenders because they know they can get away with it

"Activists are seen as fronting foreign views and opinions, enemies of the state and enemies of development."

Amanzuru, who won the EU Human Rights Defenders Award in 2019, says environmental abuse in Uganda is highly militarised, so any intervention for nature conservation seems like a battlefield in a highly sophisticated war.

"You directly deal with our finest military elite who run the show because of the huge profits gained from it," he said. "We are always being followed by state and non-state actors and those involved in the depletion of natural resources like the Zoka Central Forest Reserve."

Amanzuru said he had received threatening phone calls and had been intimidated by government and local police officials. "My phone is always tapped," he added.

Anthony Masake, programme officer at Chapter Four Uganda, a human rights organisation, said environmental human rights defenders in Uganda were increasingly operating in a hostile environment.

"They repeatedly face reprisal attacks in the form of arbitrary arrests and detention, character assassination, being labelled traitors, assaults, intimidation and isolation, among others," he said.

Masake added that illegal loggers and charcoal dealers, land grabbers and corporations often connived with their government backers to shield them from the law and accountability.

"Politicians, police officers and local leaders have often been cited in incidents of reprisal attacks against environmental defenders in Adjumani, Hoima and other districts," he said.

Uganda's environmental battlefields

are located in rural and remote areas where life and time seem to stop – far from the public eye and the noise and the vibe of big cities.

"The terrain has exposed them to easy targeting because the operation areas are far removed from urban areas where they would be able to access quick and competent legal services," said Masake.

ABOVE: A timber truck in Uganda, 2009.

"The rise of incidents of corruption, abuse of office, lack of accountability for abusers and deterioration of the state and rule of law has further emboldened perpetrators to continue attacking environmental defenders because they know they can get away with it."

As watchdogs of society, journalists who attempt to expose environmental crimes and abuse are also often the victims of sheer brutality and violence, according to several sources who spoke to Index.

"I deplore the way [president Yoweri] Museveni's security forces ill-treat journalists, especially environmental journalists," said one. "They have done nothing wrong. All they do is to tell the nation and the world that our natural resources are in danger of being extinct if we do not trade carefully. Is that a crime?"

The journalist, who claimed to fear Ugandan security forces and ➔

All hell broke loose when security forces arrested more environmental activists

→ intelligence services "more than God", spoke only on condition of anonymity.

The International Federation for Human Rights (FIDH) and its partners, the Observatory for the Protection of Human Rights Defenders and the World Organisation Against Torture, have vehemently and repeatedly condemned the arrest and arbitrary detention of environmental journalists.

Venex Watebawa and Joshua Mutale, the team leader and head of programmes at Water and Environment Media Network (WEMNET), were recently arrested in Hoima, in western Uganda, on their way to attend a radio talkshow at Spice FM.

The FIDH reported that they were supposed to discuss the risks and dangers of sugarcane growing projects in the Bugoma forest and of allowing oil activities in critical biodiversity areas including rivers, lakes, national parks, forests and wetlands.

Home to more than 600 chimpanzees and endangered bird species, including African grey parrots, Bugoma is a tropical rainforest which was declared as a nature reserve in 1932.

Following the arrest of WEMNET members, all hell broke loose

ABOVE: William Amanzuru

when security forces arrested more environmental activists who went to the police station to negotiate the release of Watebawa and Mutale.

The arrests, which are believed to have been called for by Hoima Sugar, the company decimating the Bugoma forest to convert it into a sugarcane plantation, were a bitter pill to swallow.

"Environment stories are so delicate because the people behind the destruction of the environment are people with a lot of money, who are well connected and have a lot of influence," Watebawa told Index.

He slammed the National Environment Management Authority – which is mandated to oversee conservation efforts – for having been influenced by Hoima Sugar.

"To our surprise, it gave a report in a record time of two weeks to clear the below-bare-minimum-standard environmental impact assessment report to clear 22 square miles of land in a sensitive and fragile ecosystem," he said.

"The deployment of paramilitary agencies to give sanctuary to the destroyers of the forest speaks volumes of the government's commitment to protect the environment."

Journalists who have attempted to get anywhere near the Bugoma central forests have been harassed or faced the wrath of the army.

"These incidents have demotivated and scared us," said Watebawa. "Between March and June, two of our members lost their cameras and laptops. Our communications officer, Samuel Kayiwa, was trailed, his car broken into in Kajjasi, and his gear stolen."

In another incident targeting the environmental media, Wemnet reported that someone broke into the house of Agnes Nantambi, a journalist working

for New Vision, after midnight, forcing her to surrender her laptop and camera.

Amanzuru was arrested in February after an incident in which locals impounded a Kampala-bound truck ferrying illegal charcoal. He claimed that the military provided protection for those investing in illegal logging, illegal timber harvesting and the commercial charcoal trade.

He said the country's environment sector was highly politicised, with the government drawing a lot of illicit money from the abuse of natural resources.

"Politicians trade in environmental abuse because this is an unmonitored trade ... They make quick money for their political sustainability."

And as the Museveni government's aggression towards environmental activists increases day by day, human rights organisations have vowed to fight and to die with their boots on.

Amanzuru's arrest attracted the attention of the EU ambassador to Uganda, who wrote to environment minister Beatrice Anywar Atim to request a fair and speedy trial.

Entities offering support include the Defenders' Protection Initiative, Chapter Four Uganda and the National Coalition of Human Rights Defenders in Uganda.

But despite the grim outlook, Watebawa remains optimistic about the future of environmental activism.

He says society is stronger, more organised and more determined than ever, and the media persistently exposes environmental abuse.

He believes all responsible citizens must challenge the impunity to which environmental human rights defenders so often fall victim because the environment, ultimately, is a shared resource. ✖

Issa Sikiti da Silva is an Index contributing editor based in West Africa

Index asked Hoima Sugar to comment on these allegations but received no response.

50(03):64/66|DOI:10.1177/03064220211048864

COMMENT

"Anarchic, ecstatic behaviour, at least in a limited form,
should not be discouraged and certainly not stamped on"

MARK GLANVILLE ON THE OPPROBRIUM HE RECEIVED FROM EQUATING FOOTBALL HOOLIGANS
WITH THE MAENADS OF ANCIENT GREEK MYTHOLOGY | BETTER OUT THAN IN? P78

Cigar smoke and mirrors

Cuba's PR spinners may paint a pretty picture but, says **JAMES BLOODWORTH**, things are not always as they may seem

THE CUBAN REVOLUTION has always been adept at PR. Even in the early days of the guerrilla struggle, before the revolution succeeded in overthrowing the brutal USA-backed dictator Fulgencio Batista, Cuban rebel leader Fidel Castro was a master of propaganda.

When US journalist Herbert Matthews visited the Sierra Maestra in 1957 and sat down with Castro for an interview, the comandante fooled Matthews into thinking rebel forces were stronger than they were by marching the same columns of men past at various intervals and having "messengers" return to report the existence of non-existent rebel units.

"From the look of things, General Batista cannot possibly hope to suppress the Castro revolt," wrote the New York Times correspondent in his subsequent dispatch.

Over the ensuing half-century, Havana's propaganda has been equally powerful – bolstering an image abroad of Cuba as a besieged outpost against US

aggression; a beacon of healthcare and education; and a country where children are taught to live lives of ascetic self-sacrifice in emulation of revolutionary icon Ernesto "Che" Guevara (who, like Castro, is the subject of a cult of personality in Cuba).

For those living at a distance from the Cuban reality, it is easy to be taken in by the idealistic penumbra that surrounds the revolution. The arbitrary arrests, the grinding poverty, the oppression that reaches into every corner of daily life – all are submerged in the minds of foreign admirers beneath a tide of olive-green, cigar-burnished kitsch.

Yet as thousands of Cubans take to the country's dilapidated streets in unprecedented protests against the dictatorship, it is important that Western human rights and free speech organisations do not allow this popular yet grossly distorted image of Cuba to muddy their thinking.

Many have not. Each year, Amnesty International produces a detailed and damning appraisal of the human rights situation in Cuba. In its 2020 report, Amnesty noted that the authorities in Havana "continued to repress all forms of dissent, including by imprisoning independent artists, journalists and members of the political opposition".

Since the mass protests began on 11 July, Amnesty has been closely monitoring the situation on the island, publishing regular updates as to the whereabouts of Cuban activists and dissident voices.

Human Rights Watch has produced similarly comprehensive reports

ABOVE: A mural in Havana by artist and social critic Fabian Lopez, 2019

in its coverage of the deteriorating situation in Cuba for opponents of the dictatorship. And Reporters Without Borders has condemned the repression of citizen protests.

Despite this mounting evidence that the government in Havana is an egregious violator of human rights, and despite the landmark protests by thousands of Cubans who risk imprisonment by marching in the streets and demanding "libertad" (freedom), one senses that Cuba is unlikely to become a cause célèbre among progressive activists in the way that Palestine, or even Belarus, have.

Worse, some left-wing organisations in the USA and the UK, ostensibly dedicated to human rights and firmly embedded in the social democratic institutions of their countries, have openly backed the dictatorship. The Democratic Socialists of America, Young Labour, Black Lives Matter and Progressive International have all

For those living at a distance from the Cuban reality, it is easy to be taken in by the idealistic penumbra that surrounds the revolution

ABOVE: A policeman watches on as protesters stage a rare sight of discontent in Havana in a demonstration against Cuban President Miguel Diaz-Canel. July 11, 2021

released statements in support of the government in Havana.

Ordinary Cubans have had to put up with similar condescension projected onto their island by preening academics and intellectuals who have lived cossetted lives in liberal democracies for many decades.

In his memoir, Before Night Falls, the exiled Cuban writer Reinaldo Arenas, who was sentenced to hard labour by the communist regime for his homosexuality and for his critical writings, used the term "communist deluxe" to describe such people.

In his book he writes of a German professor who, at a Harvard University banquet, informed him that, despite the hardships Arenas may personally have suffered, the professor was a "great admirer of Fidel Castro" and

"very happy with what he has done in Cuba". The professor said this between mouthfuls of a huge plate of food.

"I think it's fine for you to admire Fidel Castro, but in that case, you should not continue eating that food on your plate," responded Arenas. "No one in Cuba can eat food like that, with the exception of Cuban officials."

Arenas then snatched the man's plate away from him and launched it against a nearby wall.

Such encounters with ordinary Cubans are mercifully rare for foreign apologists of the dictatorship, who have failed over 62 years to learn that the red apple of Havana is rotten. They see no distinction in Cuba, which resembles a military garrison as much as a country, between the oppressed and the oppressor. Cuba is the revolution, and the revolution is Cuba. Or, as Fidel himself once put it: "Inside the revolution, everything; outside it, nothing."

The voices of ordinary Cubans are submerged under an intoxicating blend of cigars, mojitos and summer socialism.

Amid so much willed historical ignorance it is vital that organisations dedicated to free speech and human rights work to draw attention to the deteriorating situation in Cuba. As I write these words, trials have already begun against those who dared to take to the streets to call for change.

These trials are invariably followed by speedy convictions in arbitrary court proceedings which are a degradation of justice. According to groups tracking the arrests, as of 26 July nearly 700 Cubans have been detained since protests began..

It is important, too, that liberal-minded people take the reports that such

organisations produce seriously – at least as seriously as they do when the same accusations of human rights abuses are levelled at less fashionable (and less PR-savvy) dictatorships.

The Cubans I speak to are tired – tired of the indignities at the hands of the dictatorship, tired of the daily struggle to source basic commodities in an economy governed by archaic doctrines imported decades ago from a country that no longer exists.

But they are also tired of being treated as the living inhabitants of a socialist theme park, instrumentalised to serve the fantasies of those foreign admirers who carry with them a baggage of excuses for the Castroist dictatorship. As Orwell once put it, "to be corrupted by totalitarianism one does not have to live in a totalitarian country".

During the Covid-19 pandemic, many liberal and progressive voices have been quick to share news stories featuring battalions of heroic Cuban doctors being sent around the world to assist in medical efforts to beat the virus.

It would be nice if such interest in Cuba were less ephemeral; if it looked beyond Havana's carefully manufactured PR operation; and if it expressed itself, for once, by listening to what Cubans themselves were saying about the decrepit dictatorship whose tentacles extend into every aspect of their lives. ✖

James Bloodworth is a journalist, former editor of Labour blog Left Foot Forward, *and author of* Hired: Six Months Undercover in Low-Wage Britain

50(03):68/69|DOI:10.1177/03064220211048866

Denialism is not protected speech

OZ KATERJI says war crimes revisionists want us to believe they are the ones being silenced

N THE SUMMER 2021 issue of Index, Nerma Jelacic of the Commission for International Justice and Accountability argued that robust academic debate did not include space for incitement, and that the poisonous slander deployed by war crimes revisionists "puts a target on the backs" of journalists, activists and medics working in active conflict zones.

The response to Jelacic's piece from some members of the highly organised war crimes denial collective she described was as predictable as it was absurd. By demanding the right of reply they seek to present lies, fabrications and distortions as being of equal value to first-hand witness testimonies.

The job of a freedom-of-speech campaigner is not to provide an equal platform for the oppressor and the oppressed. It is to advocate on behalf of those who face persecution for speaking at all. There can be no comparison made between the survivors of crimes against humanity and those who would seek to absolve the perpetrators of these crimes.

One of the most frequent misconceptions surrounding the debate around free speech is that it is a debate about the right to a platform. A Holocaust denier is no more entitled to a microphone than an arsonist is to a box of matches.

Brutal civil wars, rising authoritarianism and violent crackdowns against political opposition groups are a daily reality for many people around the globe and free expression is under attack in Syria, Myanmar, Iran, Saudi Arabia and Russia. In some of these places, even mild public criticism of the government can be a death sentence.

Jelacic's assertion about the targeting of these regimes' critics is absolutely right, and totalitarian dictatorships have invested billions of dollars in the production and dissemination of propaganda and atrocity denial.

Agitprop is big business in 2021, with Russia Today, Press TV and CGTN being the leading names in the propaganda industry, disseminating authoritarian lies in the service of oppressive regimes – all in English, of course, because the audiences for these performances are never domestic.

Indeed, the Bashar al-Assad regime, like many others before it, made a concerted effort to target journalists to prevent the truth from getting out of Syria.

In the cases of Sunday Times journalist Marie Colvin and French photographer Remi Ochlik, the price for reporting the truth on the regime's assault on Homs was paid with their lives – a price that thousands of Syrian journalists and political activists have also paid.

In the modern age, an act as simple as objectively reporting the reality of the situation on the ground in a conflict potentially carries a death sentence. Telling the truth should not need to be a revolutionary and dangerous act of defiance, but this is where we are.

Free speech is a pressing global issue in places where the free press, freedom of expression and the right to political assembly are curtailed.

The revisionists want you to believe in the fantasy that they are being silenced.

They do this even while being paraded on huge platforms to perform their revisionist routines by the state media networks of countries that routinely imprison their own citizens for the most minor instances of political dissent.

Those who were lucky enough to escape Assad's torture chambers, starvation sieges, carpet bombing and chemical weapons are forced to relive their trauma by the barbarism and inhumanity of a handful of conspiracy theorists who have created a cottage industry out of denying their suffering.

This is an industry that has long thrived on the political fringes, and to understand the story of Syrian atrocity revisionism one need look no further than the Balkan wars – and Cambodia before that, and the Holocaust before that. Denialism will always find fertile ground in the realms of human conflict.

But this three-ring circus is, and has always been, a charade to obfuscate the simple truth. The people being silenced in this debate are the survivors of Assad's atrocities in Syria, in the same way as the survivors of these other conflicts were.

It is to those people we should be passing the microphone: people for whom freedom of speech is a life-and-death issue, not those who demand a pedestal for their unsubstantiated crankery.

In doing so, we can also seek to build solidarity with and empower survivors, as has already been displayed in recent years by Srebrenica and Holocaust memorial organisations publishing work on Syria.

Confronting denialism is, unfortunately, a tragic bond that survivors now share, but it is at least one we can help unburden them from.

The founding charter of the UN says "never again". We already owe these survivors a debt we can never repay. The very least we can do is provide them the platforms they need to testify against their oppressors and defend their integrity against those who stand against them. ✖

Oz Katerji is a British-Lebanese freelance writer and filmmaker focusing on conflict, human rights and the Middle East

50(03):70/71|DOI:10.1177/03064220211048867

Permissible weapons

PETER HITCHENS responds to Nerma Jelacic on her claims of disinformation in Syria

NERMA JELACIC, IN her recent article for Index on Censorship says there is an 'ever-expanding parachute of academic freedom and freedom of expression'. You could have fooled me, but Jelacic sounds as if she dislikes these freedoms because they shelter people she condemns.

This is a tenable position, and many people have held it down the ages. Almost anyone connected with any great enterprise has been tempted by the idea that a higher good requires the silencing of those who say things which are inconvenient to it. Many of us have also been unwilling, at some point, to accept the truth of information published by those whom we hate or despise, even if that information is true. These are interesting questions with awkward answers, but is a magazine devoted to opposing censorship the right place for such an argument, made with such fury?

I felt that the tone of Jelacic's article was that of a prosecutor at a show trial, denouncing the accused to a tribunal whose verdict was not in doubt. Take for example: "the disinformation movement has brought together a diverse coalition of leftists, communists, racists, ideologues, anti-Semites and fascists". This drips with guilt by association. Abuse of this kind is not debate. It is meant to frighten and isolate its targets, and fear is one of the most powerful means of imposing censorship.

Those she actually names in her attack can and no doubt will defend themselves. They are not my political allies and I differ from them in several important opinions. But on one thing I have found myself on the same side, and that is what I shall politely call the alleged doctoring of reports from Syria by the UN Chemical Weapons watchdog, the OPCW. Jelacic writes: "The OPCW was portrayed to be issuing doctored reports in support of the alleged Western imperialist agenda to overthrow the [Syrian] regime, including by the use of military intervention for which chemical weapons attacks would be a pretext. The disinformationists parroted Damascus and Moscow in whose view all of the alleged chemical attacks were staged on the orders of the West".

After all the foregoing fury, I was braced for a personal attack. I am perhaps the most prominent publiciser of doubts about recent OPCW reports, having done so in a large-circulation mainstream British national newspaper. If I venture on to Twitter, many people confidently shower me with slime of this sort. Yet none came from Jelacic. Perhaps this is because I am rather demonstrably not a leftist, communist, racist, ideologue, anti-Semite or fascist.

I have not suggested that the alleged attacks were staged, let alone that this was done on the orders of the West. I do not parrot Moscow or Damascus. I took up the case because, unlike almost any other journalists known to me, I read the OPCW reports with care, and then wrote about them on my Mail on Sunday blog. This led to my making direct contact with OPCW inspectors who, noting my

ABOVE: The headquarters of the OPCW in The Hague

detailed doubts, wished to tell me that they were justified and that something disturbing was indeed happening.

These decent, honest, non-political people have an important story to tell. Unlike me, they are unused to the hurly-burly of controversy, to being called foul names and accused of being the tools of foreign tyrannies. They are upset by insinuations that they acted for money or told untruths, when they did neither. They are beyond doubt intimidated by the sort of language Jelacic and others employ in this controversy. They are, in a way, censored. I have little doubt that the failure of many reporters to examine what they say impartially and properly is a direct consequence of the hurricane of abuse ("War crimes denier!" "Assad apologist!" "Tool of the Kremlin!") which is hurled at anyone who dissents from the official line. Had these methods of control been as well-developed in 2003 as they are now, we might never have known that Hussein had no WMDs. You can believe that this form of discourse is a permissible weapon. Or you can believe that censorship is wrong. But you cannot believe both. ✖

Peter Hitchens is a columnist for The Mail on Sunday

☰ Denialism will always find fertile ground in the realms of human conflict

50(03):72/72|DOI:10.1177/03064220211048868

A riveting investigation into a nightmare Orwellian social experiment

In an expose that is as timely as it is alarming, Geoffrey Cain shows how China is using artificial intelligence and totalitarian repression to turn its westernmost region into a human rights hellhole."

–BLAINE HARDEN,
author of *Escape from Camp 14*

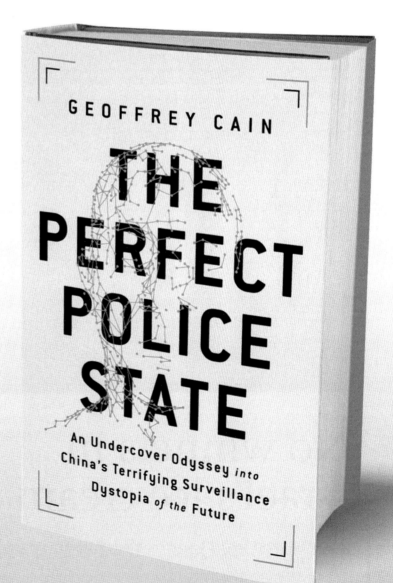

GEOFFREY CAIN

THE PERFECT POLICE STATE

An Undercover Odyssey into China's Terrifying Surveillance Dystopia of the Future

'AILABLE IN HARDCOVER
ID EBOOK FROM

PUBLICAFFAIRS

vw.publicaffairsbooks.com

No winners in Israel's ice cream war

JO-ANN MORT says the boycott movement is silencing the very people it seeks to help

ABOVE: Protestors gather in front of a Ben & Jerry's store after the ice cream company joined the Boycott, Divestment and Sanctions (BDS) movement

There is a critical difference between using boycotts or divestment to protest a government's policy and the BDS movement's goals and tactics

In late July, the Ben and Jerry's board announced it would withdraw its licensing agreement from the businessman who has held the Israeli franchise since 2000. It made this move because the Israeli licence holder was also marketing to the Jewish settlements in the Occupied Palestinian West Bank and East Jerusalem (OPT).

The board said it had intended to divest totally from Israel in line with BDS. But Unilever, which owns the ice cream company, one-upped its subsidiary by shifting the intent of the announcement to say that the company would withdraw only from supplying the Jewish settlements in the OPT, while remaining in Israel proper. The company now will try to secure a different licensing agreement if the current licensee refuses to exempt the Jewish settlements in the OPT.

While the distinction is an important one, it will prove difficult under Israeli law. That's because the previous government, under Benjamin Netanyahu, passed a law to blur the Green Line – the internationally recognised border of Israel – incorporating a ban on the banning of Israeli Jewish settlers from businesses and marketing.

Ben Cohen and Jerry Greenfield, who sold their eponymous company to Unilever in 2000, weighed in supporting the decision to halt sales in Jewish settlements in the OPT. "It's possible to support Israel and oppose some of its policies, just as we've opposed policies of the US government," they wrote in a New York Times opinion piece that also expressed their "love" for Israel, something completely anathema to the

BDS movement. Even so, the movement hailed the ice cream maker's move.

There is precedence for this type of practice, including two major EU agreements with Israel – science funding via the EU's Horizon 2020 project and a new cultural grant, both of which stipulate that Israel can't use the funds outside the Green Line.

The Israeli citizen who owns the franchise for McDonald's in Israel has long refused to put a fast-food outlet outside the Green Line. An early supporter of the anti-occupation group Peace Now, the McDonald's licensee, Omri Padan, has always been clear on where he sells his kosher Big Macs.

There is a critical difference between using boycotts or divestment to protest a government's policy and the BDS movement's goals and tactics, which encompass anything Israel or anyone Israeli. The movement makes no distinction between the Occupied West Bank or East Jerusalem or blockaded Gaza and Israel proper. It doesn't merely protest policies. It protests the existence of the state of Israel.

It calls for an end to oppression of the Palestinian people with full rights, with no equal recognition for the rights of the Jewish people who are Israeli citizens. Increasingly, it makes no distinction between the Palestinians under occupation in the West Bank, East Jerusalem and Gaza and the more than 20% of the Palestinian citizens of Israel who live inside the Green Line (and many of whom call themselves Arab citizens, not Palestinians).

The South African boycott movement, upon which BDS claims to be based, aimed to end the egregious →

BEIT ZAYIT, ISRAEL. Perhaps it isn't surprising that the ice cream wars heated up amid the dogged July heat. But it was also a stark illustration of perception versus reality in the attempt by the Boycott, Divestment, Sanctions (BDS) movement to freeze Israel out of global engagement.

→ policy of apartheid but not to delegitimise a country's very existence. Rather than support two states for two peoples, the BDS movement aims for one state. BDS regards any Jewish-Israeli institution – and increasingly any prominent Jewish-Israeli individual – as a legitimate boycott target.

BDS believes that all universities are complicit in the occupation. All arts institutions. Independent artists. Independent club owners. Independent writers. Privately-owned companies.

Swept up in this dismissal of all things Israeli are the Israeli citizens who are of Arab or Palestinian descent. As one Israeli citizen who is an Arab activist from Hadash, the communist-influenced party, said to me: "We are being ignored, too." So is the struggling peace camp and artists of all types, most of whom are opposed to their government's policies.

The impact on universities is especially ironic. Under the Netanyahu administration, the board of all university presidents in Israel voted against certifying Ariel College as a university, due to it being outside the Green Line in the settlement of Ariel, near Nablus. (The decision was overridden by the government.)

Israeli universities increasingly have significant numbers of Arab students both from within Israel and from the West Bank and East Jerusalem. (The Israeli blockade of Gaza combined with Hamas rule makes it nearly impossible for students from Gaza to enter Israel.) Haifa University's student population is nearly 40% Arab; 22% of undergraduates at Technion – considered the leading maths and science university in Israel – are Arab; 33% of graduate students in several Tel Aviv University

programmes are Arab; and, increasingly, the Hebrew University of Jerusalem has not only Arab-Israeli citizens but students from East Jerusalem and the West Bank.

Similarly, while the numbers are much lower among faculty, they are rising. But even though the previous dean of the Hebrew University Law School was an Arab citizen of Israel, the school – a bastion of human rights teaching – is on the BDS boycott list.

Noam Chomsky put it this way in an al-Jazeera interview: "The settlements and the occupation are illegal acts. Actions against these, I support... It is a mistake to go broader to arts, culture, universities – I don't advocate targeting Harvard University, even though the USA is involved in horrific acts."

Another active leftist, the musician Steve Earle, has been to Israel twice – once to perform and once for a week to co-produce an album for Israeli-Jewish musician David Broza in an East Jerusalem, Palestinian-owned studio. He was quoted in a Nation magazine interview about why he was against cultural boycotts: "I do more good when I go and see what I see and I come back and I sing about it."

The BDS movement can claim success in making it so difficult for several prominent musicians to perform in Israel that some have pulled out of concerts, some at the last minute. It's a small market and if it becomes too much of a hassle, it's easier for musicians to cancel or avoid booking.

In one case where I was working with the musician, the result was that the private indie rock club took a tremendous financial loss when he pulled out at the last minute due to social media pressure. The musician decided

to visit on his own and learn more about the situation between Israel and the Palestinians. But he didn't perform and the loss wasn't recouped for the club. How was this a victory for the Palestinian people?

There are numerous examples of performers being convinced not to visit, but it's worth highlighting one case of someone who did travel. Leonard Cohen was set to perform in Israel in 2009, even though BDS activists in Ramallah protested against his visit.

Cohen's manager, Robert Kory, told the Associated Press: "There are a lot of people who don't want us here, and anything done here invites controversy. But we believe freedom of speech is very, very important."

Cohen left the region after using the proceeds from the concert to establish the Fund for Reconciliation, Tolerance and Peace. Most of the money was earmarked to support the Parents Circle, a group of Jewish-Israeli and Palestinian parents whose families had died in the conflict.

This example could be a template for a different way to use the power of the arts – to engage debate rather than stifle it.

BDS activism has been growing on social media, where it seems to have the most impact. But the Israeli economy is thriving, even amid Covid-19. Israel's largest trading partner, the EU, will never cut ties with the country, even as it has tried to force Israel to label or separate goods made in the Jewish settlements.

As I write this article, the Israeli foreign minister is planning a public visit to Morocco and planes have begun flying direct between the two countries for the first time. With a new government in Israel comprising left, right and centre, two Israeli ministers have met their Palestinian counterparts for the first time in years.

The psychological impact of these changes on Israel, especially the Jewish majority, has been intense. Yet there is something missing. Voices unheard

 BDS regards any Jewish-Israeli institution – and increasingly any prominent Jewish-Israeli individual – as a legitimate target

This example could be a template for a different way to use the power of the arts – to engage debate rather than stifle it

in Israel from Palestine and Palestine's supporters would be an important addition to the debate, were they allowed to be heard.

There's another reason for the psychological reaction inside Israel and within the global Jewish community. Boycotts against the Jewish people are loaded with horrific historic precedent,

dating back to the late 1800s in Germany, spreading through Europe and culminating in the Holocaust. Exclusion from professional guilds was a norm in many places.

It's nearly impossible to see how the BDS movement can have the ultimate impact it desires. It will never cause Israel to change policy and it will certainly never erase Israel as a Jewish state. It won't even aid those

inside Israel who are trying to build an anti-occupation or anti-racist camp to develop a stronger shared society between Jewish-Israelis and the Arab minority. But, in the meantime, the silence of those who could grow the chorus inside Israel against the occupation is deafening. ✖

Jo-Ann Mort writes frequently about Israel and Palestine, most recently for Dissent (where she is an editorial board member), The American Prospect, and The New York Review of Books Daily. She lives in New York but travels to the region frequently. Twitter: @changecommnyc

50(03):74/77|DOI:10.1177/03064220211048872

ABOVE: Arab students at Tel Aviv University

Better out than in?

MARK GLANVILLE says today's thuggery on the terraces has a lot in common with historical social safety valves and the rites and revelry of ancient times

FOLLOWING THE EXPLOITS of certain rowdy elements before and after the England v Italy final at Euro 2000, The Sunday Times asked me to write a reflective piece on football hooliganism based on my 50-year involvement in that world.

One paragraph in my piece read:

"To refer to the classics, like the Bacchae in Euripides, they lose the shackles of civilisation, connecting to deep, repressed parts of the human psyche that needed expression and recognition."

In more than 200 online comments I was pilloried as a psychopath, a sociopath, an idiot who should be in prison and a disgrace to my father and the Jewish people.

Some excoriated The Sunday Times for publishing the article. Others said they had cancelled their subscriptions. Among my detractors was a lady who wrote: "This made me cringe – especially the part about the Bacchae. What next? Rapists are fine because of Zeus and Europa?"

"Sod the Bacchae," another added.

But in the Bacchae, I believe, lies a good explanation for the phenomenon of football hooliganism.

A healthy society recognises the need for its members to access coping

mechanisms that help them survive the controls necessary to make that society function. Confident, open societies license certain drugs and activities, the panem et circenses which allow their members to let off steam.

Less confident, oppressive societies outlaw them. The Taliban recently humiliated and executed the comedian Nazar Mohammad, better known as Khasha Zwan, after a video emerged of him being abused by them. (Dictators don't like being laughed at, as exiled Soviet poet Osip Mandelstam discovered.)

As a warning to overly rule-bound societies, The Bacchae, Euripides's remarkable final play, first performed in Athens in 405 BCE, supplies the urtext. Dionysus, god of wine and other ecstasy-inducing substances and activities, arrives from Asia attended by his band of Bacchae (also known as Maenads), female revellers high on the drink and dance integral to his rites.

In Thebes they are confronted by the city's ruler, King Pentheus, who is deeply alarmed to see the citizens of Thebes, members of his own family included, drawn into this rowdy cult.

Pentheus arrests Dionysus, who is disguised as a stranger, but the god's magic is too powerful for a mortal ruler to contain. Dionysus, sometimes known as Lusios (the liberator), frees himself and destroys the king's palace with earthquake and fire. He then asks Pentheus if he would like to see what the Bacchae get up to on Mount Cithaeron.

Pentheus cannot contain his voyeuristic curiosity. With little encouragement, he dresses up as a woman so he can pass himself off as one of the Bacchae and spy on their activities. Once on Cithaeron, Dionysus

leads Pentheus to a horrific fate – torn limb from limb by Bacchae led by his own mother, Agave.

Dionysus represents the ecstatic, anarchic element of the human psyche that one suppresses at one's peril. In The Bacchae he is nature, red in tooth and claw. It is telling that his destruction of Pentheus and what he stands for

Is there a lost ritual that has allowed football hooliganism to develop and thrive?

ABOVE: Russian and Polish fans fight at Euro 2012

– man's attempt to control not only the behaviour of men but nature itself – is initiated with the uncontrollable natural phenomenon of an earthquake.

Dionysus's terrible vengeance on the symbol of law and order in The Bacchae – Pentheus, King of Thebes – is a warning to all who would repress the outlets needed to survive social repression. The Bacchae's message is that anarchic, ecstatic behaviour, at least in a limited form, should not be discouraged, and certainly not stamped on. It is part of who we are.

Let us drink, dance and play the tambourine. If not, we might start indulging in genuinely anti-social behaviour, such as tearing people apart or fighting at football matches.

Football hooligans, their antics often fuelled by drugs and alcohol, have a lot in common with the Bacchae.

The police, representatives of law and order, are a sworn enemy.   →

ABOVE: An England fan ascends a lamppost in Leicester Square, before the Euro 2020 final, July 2021

→ In turn, the police regard football hooligans as a criminal, anti-social element to be repressed and imprisoned.

In the UK, those involved in football violence receive more severe sentences than those breaking the same laws in a different context, such as at the pub on a Saturday night.

Football hooligan conspiracy (arranging a fight in advance) is met with especially severe penalties. A Burnley hooligan received a five-year sentence for organising a fight with rivals that did not even take place!

Conspiracy is redolent of secretive, underground societies. The mysteries of cults, from the Bacchae of Asia to the Millwall Bushwackers, make them seem more dangerous and troubling still to non-initiates such as Pentheus and the police.

ER Dodds, the great Greek scholar and commentator on Bacchae, distinguished between the black, destructive Maenadism practised by the Bacchae in Thebes as a consequence of repression – "a punishment upon the too respectable" – and the white Maenadism of ordered ritual described in the choral ode at the beginning of the play, which he believed was derived from an actual Bacchic hymn sung by celebrants.

Oh
Blessed is he who, happy one,
knows the rites of the gods,
lives purely and
initiates his soul in the Bacchic revels.

The Tarantism of Puglia – arguably a direct descendant of the Dionysiac rites practised by that region's locals at the time Bacchae was written – might also be seen as a ritual catharsis conducted according to certain rules and customs.

Taranta culture evolved in medieval times as a cure for people, usually

women, who had apparently been poisoned by the tarantula bite.

Most researchers in the field have concluded that there never was a spider. These were women suffering from depression in a patriarchal, repressive society, their symptoms relieved by dancing to an ecstasy-inducing rhythm.

Watching Taranta, Gianfranco Mingozzi's extraordinary 1962 film documenting the final throes of the tradition, you also see how ritualised the process of curing afflicted women was.

The band plays set melodies, the woman mimics the movements of the spider that supposedly bit her and an icon of St Paul, patron saint of the

tarantulas ever since the tradition was commandeered by the Catholic church, oversees proceedings.

Each year, on 29 June, those suffering from this illness – known as tarantism – gathered to be cured in the Church of St Peter and St Paul in Galatina.

As the society that gave rise to it became more enlightened, the tradition died, and its music has become an entertainment.

Performing it in London clubs with my group, Amaraterra, one sees how joyful it makes people looking for release from the stresses of modern urban life today. It is a safety valve, offering brief, harmless escape from an over-ordered society.

But ecstatic dance in an uncontrolled, non-ritual environment, as with the Bacchae, has historically led to dance crazes, such as those of post-Depression America and 14th century Germany following the Black Death.

Like football hooliganism, they are what Dodds would call black Maenadism. Some football thugs even refer to fighting as "dancing".

Is there a lost ritual that has allowed football hooliganism to thrive? It started to evolve around the time National Service was no longer obligatory – an environment in which young, testosterone-charged men had their aggression channelled in a ritualised, disciplined way. Is that a coincidence?

Dodds wrote: "If I understand early Dionysiac ritual aright, its social function was essentially cathartic, in the psychological sense. It purged the individual of those infectious irrational impulses which, when dammed up, had given rise, as they have done in other cultures, to outbreaks of dancing mania and similar manifestations of collective hysteria; it relieved them by providing them with a ritual outlet."

Ritual is, arguably, another form of social control, but by channelling hysterical and destructive impulses, it provides a harmless outlet for them.

My Sunday Times article was

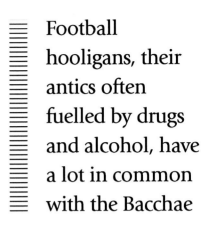

Football hooligans, their antics often fuelled by drugs and alcohol, have a lot in common with the Bacchae

intended not only to challenge its readers but to provoke their curiosity.

Interestingly, as well as receiving a shoal of negative, mostly ad hominem, criticism, it was also the fifth most-read article in the paper that day.

"It's left me feeling strangely odd – part disgusted, part despairing and part weary. It's rare to get a glimpse inside the mind of the type of person I despise, and I'm now feeling like I should have a hot shower and scrub myself clean. No thanks to the Times team for this one," wrote one lady, perhaps a latter-day Pentheus curious to get a glimpse into an elemental part of herself that she would rather was left untouched.

Some were critical of The Sunday Times for publishing my article at all. Was I saying the unsayable? Is it better not to dig too deeply into those areas of ourselves, for fear we may stumble upon an elemental place that the rule-obeying part of our psyche is unable to control?

Dodds was in no doubt. "To resist Dionysus is to repress the elemental in one's own nature; the punishment is the sudden complete collapse of the inward dykes when the elemental breaks through perforce and civilisation vanishes."

As someone replying to the shower lady pointed out: "If it is true, it shows what civilisation is up against." ✖

Mark Glanville is a writer and singer

50(03):78/81|DOI:10.1177/03064220211048873

Russia's great export: hostility to the free press

MIKHAIL KHORDOKOVSKY writes about how autocratic countries are using everything from forced incarceration in psychiatric wards to banning journalism itself

THREE YEARS AGO, on 30 July 2019, the Russian journalists Orkhan Dzhemal, Aleksandr Rastogruev and Kirill Radchenko were brutally murdered in the Central African Republic while making a documentary about the dealings of military contractors Wagner Group. No official investigation of that crime took place, no justice was served to the criminals, and despite the independently collected evidence indicating the murderers, they are still enjoying impunity. On 30 July 2021, access to the Dossier Center website was blocked in Russia by a Moscow court request; the outlet had previously released an investigation into the journalists' murder.

This dire situation is not unique to authoritarian countries like the Central African Republic or Russia. Murders, beatings, cyber-attacks, death threats, online abuse and repressive legislation are just a few of the methods used to silence journalists, hide the truth and deprive the public of the right to know.

According to data collected by the Justice for Journalists Foundation (JFJ) - an organisation created by my business partner and I as a tool to fight crimes against media workers worldwide - between 2017 till today, over 12,000 attacks on media workers took place in the 12 post-Soviet states, including 2,270 attacks in 2021. Representatives of authorities remain the main source of threats: in 57% of cases they are behind physical attacks, in 52% – non-physical and cyber-attacks and in 88% – attacks via judicial and economic means.

Although not the most common, one of the most worrying punitive measures against media workers is the tried and tested Soviet anti-dissident method of forced incarceration in psychiatric institutions. Since 2017, JFJ has recorded ten attacks of this type in Uzbekistan, Kazakhstan, Crimea, and Russia - the leader in using this inhumane method.

Increasingly, independent journalists are subjected to systematic persecution using tools from two or more categories of assaults. Azerbaijan, Belarus, Kazakhstan, Russia and Uzbekistan are among the countries that practise systematic hybrid attacks against singled-out journalists using a variety of different types of persecutions. As a result, media workers have been forced to quit the profession, emigrate or even, succumbing to intolerable pressure, take their own lives as Russia's Irina Slavina did.

Azerbaijani investigative journalist Khadija Ismayilova is one of the victims of a hybrid attack; she was threatened, harassed, attacked and sent to prison for her work in pursuing the truth about the Azerbaijani government. In 2011, after the publication of the Panama Papers, a secret camera was installed into her house and videos recorded were used to blackmail her. She was recently revealed to be one of 180 journalists worldwide targeted by the infamous Pegasus spyware, developed by the NSO Group.

In 2021, the Russian authorities have expanded the lists of "foreign agents" and "undesirable organisations", including more news outlets and journalists. The government makes it impossible for independent media workers to work there. Currently, there are 34 entities and individuals in the "foreign agent" registry, 17 of which were added in 2021.

This technique, also prevalent in Belarus, effectively prohibits media outlets from publishing anything, prevents co-operation with foreign media outlets without accreditation, levies fines in the millions if information is not removed, criminalises fake news and prosecutes of individuals and legal entities for dealing with "undesirable" or "extremist" organisations.

The harassment of journalists includes searches, seizures of personal belongings, documents and equipment, opening criminal cases on trumped-up charges, and, as ever, smear campaigns on state-owned television channels.

Most prominent Russian-language investigative and news outlets, such as Proekt, Meduza, Open Media, VTimes, The Insider and others have been forced to shut down or move abroad to continue their operations.

> Murders, beatings, cyber-attacks, death threats, online abuse are just a few of the methods used to silence journalists

Unfortunately, the pressure does not stop when journalists emigrate. Tajikistani independent journalists who were forced to leave the country still face constant pressure from the authorities. Discrediting materials are published by state TV channels and online news outlets, while journalists' relatives are prosecuted and physically attacked.

Those who are not able to leave face dire conditions. In Belarus, at least 29 media workers are awaiting trial in detention centres or under the house arrest. Belsat TV journalists Katsiaryna Bakhvalava (Andreyeva) and Darya Chultsova are already serving their two years' sentence in a penal colony. Pershiy Region correspondent Siarhei Hardziyevich was sentenced to 18 months for insulting and defaming Belarusian president Alexander Lukashenko, as well as two police officers in a Telegram chat.

It is the seemingly endless abuse of power by state authorities in countries with flawed or no democracy that is making vexatious legal threats and quasi-legal attacks against journalists virtually impossible to withstand. The Covid-19 pandemic gave rise to more anti-free speech laws and actions, and non-democratic governments embraced this pretext to enhance censorship, increase arrests of media workers, persecution and close the last remaining independent media outlets.

Turkmenistan, the dictatorship consistently rated one of the worst in the Reporters without Borders' Media Freedom ranking, demonstrates the possible climax of this trend. No independent media remains in the country, almost no independent information is coming out of it, and the only resident journalist openly cooperating with foreign outlets is 71-year-old Soltan Achilova, who is constantly subjected to beatings, detentions and other assaults.

However, it is not just the autocracies with no rule of law who are silencing all sources of independent information: we

ABOVE: Flowers near the Central House of Journalists in memory of Kirill Radchenko, Orkhan Dzhemal and Alexander Rastorguyev, murdered in the Central African Republic in 2018.

are witnessing the export of quasi-legal methods of attacks against journalists from these rogue countries to Europe and the UK. The UK legal system is increasingly used as a base of operations for judicial tourism by people of questionable morals who want to avoid publicity around their corrupt dealings. British legal and reputation-laundering companies are heavily investing their talent, influence and connections into helping them, essentially, to silence the free media worldwide.

Kremlin-affiliated businessmen are no exception. They are using the British judicial system to pursue journalists. In this context, it is noteworthy that a number of Russian businessmen and Russian affiliates are currently bringing libel proceedings against Catherine Belton in relation to her book Putins People. While this claim is still ongoing and it may be that the court will find that their complaints about the book are justified or fair, the effect of a high profile claim brought by people of enormous wealth is to make all other investgators and reporters excessively cautious.

It is crucial to know there are unlimited financial resources in the hands of their opponents, and possibly other Kremlin resources too. The public good requires particularly strong protection.

Vexatious legal threats and what have become known as strategic lawsuits against public participation (SLAPPs) are now preventing the public worldwide from knowing what they don't know. Being subjects of the litigation, journalists can't talk about their cases without facing further legal threats. although people are entitled to defend a reputation unfairly damaged, there is always a risk that the goal of some libel litigation could be far from finding jue or defending reeputattins, but to bury evidence of wrongdoing under a heep of vexatious lawsuits and demotivate other journalists.

JFJ is wholeheartedly supporting initiatives by media workers, NGOs and government institutions to enhance their expertise on the issue and doing everything possible to support the fundamental democratic institution - free and independent reporting. ✖

Mikhail Khodorkovsky is founder of the Justice for Journalists Foundation

50(03):82/83|DOI:10.1177/03064220211048874

Remembering Peter R de Vries

FREDERIKE GEERDINK celebrates the life of a Dutch journalist who spent his life investigating crime and who died after being gunned down as he left a TV studio

ON 15 JULY, Dutch crime reporter Peter R de Vries died from his injuries after being shot multiple times. The attack had taken place nine days earlier, just after he had left the studio of a TV show to which he was a regular contributor.

De Vries, who was 64 and leaves behind a partner and two children, will be remembered not only for his investigations and stories but also for the way he stood in solidarity with crime victims, deeply motivated to help them find justice. It is believed that his decision to act as the confidant of a prosecution witness in a huge organised-crime trial was behind the murder.

RTL, the station that broadcasts the daily news show RTL Boulevard, in which de Vries had appeared on the day he was attacked, said: "Peter's influence remains stronger than any act of hate can ever be. We will continue to speak freely about wrongs and injustice in society, like he did his whole life."

The Dutch Association of Editors-in-Chief said: "Peter R de Vries was an icon of Dutch journalism and an incredible support for many people. It is intensely sad that he is no longer among us. With Peter, we lost a tireless and courageous fighter for justice."

The crime beat

De Vries started his career in 1978 as a trainee journalist at De Telegraaf, the biggest newspaper in the Netherlands. He started using the "R" of his second name, Rudolf, to distinguish himself from a colleague with the same name. Crime journalism wasn't really a beat yet, but he took it up and soon published his first story about a murder.

He became famous in 1983 when he reported about the kidnapping of beer magnate Freddy Heineken. The book he published about the kidnapping a few years later remained the bestselling true crime book in the Netherlands for years.

He left the paper within a year to become the editor-in-chief of the weekly Aktueel, which he soon turned into a crime magazine. After that, he switched to TV, although he always continued to write as well.

In the early 1990s, he went freelance and started the weekly show Peter R de Vries, Crime Journalist. An episode in 2008 brought him international fame: he used an undercover reporter to trigger Joran van der Sloot, a suspect in the disappearance of US teenager Natalee Holloway on the Caribbean island of Aruba, into confessing that he was present at her death. He won an Emmy for the programme.

Another investigation revealed one of the biggest errors in Dutch judicial history: two brothers were convicted of murder, but de Vries's investigations led to a retrial and acquittal.

Apart from his investigation into the Heineken kidnapping, de Vries was not known for reporting organised crime. He mostly focused on cold cases, deceit and scams, standing beside the victims and often confronting perpetrators in

He never shied away from crossing the boundaries of journalism

front of the camera. His being there carrying out his own investigations with a thorough knowledge of both the criminal world and the justice system became a fact of life for police and prosecutors, who were also relentlessly held to account by de Vries.

He never shied away from crossing the boundaries of journalism, either: he recently started a crowdfunding campaign to raise €1 million to be used as tip money to help solve a cold case of a missing student dating back to 1983.

In the last couple of years, de Vries had become increasingly vocal about social issues in the Netherlands, speaking up for the rights of refugees and against racism. Even though he was respected and popular, his stance triggered a flood of hate and threats against him like never before, he said.

In 2016, he won an award for speaking out against racism and inequality with "courage and nerve, with arguments and substance and without fear", and that summed him up.

Looking in the mirror

After de Vries was shot, two men were arrested: a 21-year-old from Rotterdam and a 35-year-old from Poland.

It is believed that the reporter's murder is linked to the Marengo case, which revolves around a large and exceptionally violent drugs gang led by Ridouan Taghi, who was arrested in 2019. De Vries was the confidant of the prosecution witness in the case, Nabil B.

In an interview with the magazine Vrij Nederland, de Vries explained: "I couldn't have looked at myself in the mirror any more if I had refused his request. I hold the police and the prosecutor to account and I couldn't do that if I recoiled from requests for help myself, even if they involved risks."

The risk was clear: in 2018, Nabil B's brother was murdered by Taghi's men. A year later, Derk Wiersum, Nabil B's lawyer, was murdered. Despite the risk, de Vries refused personal protection.

To be accepted by the authorities and get access to his client, de Vries became an employee of the lawyer's office that represented the prosecution witness. It was a clear risk.

In the Vrij Nederland interview, de Vries said: "I'm not a scared person, but Nabil's brother and his previous lawyer were murdered so you don't have to be hysterical to think something may happen. That's part of the job. A crime reporter who thinks 'It's all getting a bit too intense now' when the going gets tough should instead work for Libelle," referring to a weekly women's magazine.

Thomas Bruning, general secretary of the Dutch Association of Journalists (NVJ), told Index: "We have to nuance the image of this being about press freedom only. Nevertheless, for his colleagues, this is an attack on one of them, and it creates a chilling climate."

This climate has become colder in the last couple of years. Research by the NVJ has shown that more journalists in the Netherlands are being targeted verbally or physically for their work.

National broadcaster NOS last year decided not to use vans with its logo any more because it was increasingly triggering aggression. On Twitter, politician Geert Wilders, leader of the Party for Freedom, recently called journalists "scum".

Bruning said: "Criminals aren't triggered by that, of course, but this all complicates the role of journalists in society. There have been threats against journalists, and now one such threat was

Before, criminals killed each other, then they murdered a lawyer, now there's been the murder of a journalist for, most likely, his role in a trial.

put into practice."

Bruning, who has discussed the issue with justice minister Ferd Grapperhaus, said there was a difference between de Vries's murder and those elsewhere,

such as the killings of Daphne Caruana Galizia in Malta in 2017 and Ján Kuciak in Slovakia in 2018, which laid bare corruption within the state.

He said: "It's positive that two suspects have been arrested. The authorities do take this seriously so I don't think we can draw a parallel with murders of journalists elsewhere."

Nevertheless, Bruning said he had told Grapperhaus that the trend was worrying. He said: "Before, criminals killed each other, then they murdered a lawyer, now a journalist for, most likely, his role in a trial.

"Who knows? Maybe the next target is a journalist who only reports about crime. It's a slippery slope." ✖

Frederike Geerdink is a Dutch freelance journalist and author.

50(03):84/85|DOI:10.1177/03064220211048875

RIGHT: Flowers, candles and messages of support for Peter R de Vries in the Lange Leidsedwarsstraat in the centre of Amsterdam on 8 July 2021 as he remaind critical in hospital

A right royal minefield

It seems that whenever members of the Royal Family are interviewed, it opens another can of worms. JOHN LLOYD wonders why.

LEFT: Princess Dian during her infamous interview with Martin Bashir, 1993

THE BRITISH ROYAL Family have been badly served by the media – and the more they give of themselves to an interviewer, the worse they seem to be treated.

In each case it has been the fault of those of them who chose to be interviewed. The example of the Japanese Imperial Family – a mystery within a ceremony, wrapped in silence – must be a tempting model.

But of course they should be interviewed. There have been interviews that have done what encounters between journalists and powerful public figures should do.

The interviewers have sought information which illuminates their subjects' actions and their beliefs, and picked up on serious allegations of misdemeanours, even crimes.

In every case, the royal interviewees accepted the interviews in order to win public support. In every case, the reverse happened and they lost much of the support they had.

The televised interview, much more than tabloid scandals, is the most treacherous of devices to use to increase or restore reputation. The tabloids can be dismissed as merely sensational (even though, if usually either fawning or bilious in their celebrity coverage, they are often broadly right). The studio interview may be full of lies or half-truths but what cannot be dismissed as

false is what the interviewee has said, which can haunt forever.

The danger of the interview is large. Yet the most famed of these interviews – that of Diana, Princess of Wales, by the BBC's Martin Bashir in 1993 – reveals a large danger for journalism, too.

* * *

In April this year, Prince Harry – Prince Charles's younger son – and his wife Meghan Markle (the Duke and Duchess of Sussex) were interviewed by Oprah Winfrey, the most popular and most highly paid interviewer on US television.

The interview was in two parts: in the first, Meghan was interviewed alone: in the second, Harry joined her and answered most of the questions. Both Oprah and the Sussexes – already some sort of friends as Oprah was invited to their wedding in May 2018 – wanted the show to happen. Indeed, the star interviewer's presence at the

wedding was a station on the road to the interview.

It was hailed as a major event, and one broadly flattering to the couple. They must have been pleased, since they spoke and tweeted enthusiastically about its impact afterwards, as did Oprah.

As time passes, however, it sinks more and more to the level of other royal interviews, which did the interviewees no favours even as they shed light on their lives.

One of Harry's answers to an Oprah question was that he had been cut off without a penny from his family in the first quarter of 2020, when the couple moved to the USA.

In June this year, his father produced evidence that he had given the couple a share of £4.452m along with his elder son, Prince William, and wife Kate – the Duke and Duchess of Cambridge.

Still, the couple implicitly acknowledged that they had received financial help, issuing a statement saying there was no contradiction in this, since Harry had meant the first quarter of 2020-21. For the sceptical, however, this statement seemed hard to square with the common-sense view of what Harry actually said and meant: no money since early 2020.

A series of claims were made, including one of racism shown to Meghan (whose mother is African-American) and of suicidal impulses prompted by this and other mistreatment by members of the royal household.

She spoke of a question asked by a member of the royal household on how dark-skinned her first child would be. Harry confirmed this, but gave no details about the person involved, or what he or she had said.

Oprah's technique was to use her large reputation to endorse the charges uncritically. Yet asking how dark skinned the child of a white man and a mixed-race woman would be is not in itself racist: it could be, were it from a hostile and racist source – or it could be simple curiosity.

The only way to know about such allegations is to know the details: the who, what, when, where and, if possible, why – the verities of free journalism everywhere.

Quite likely, the Sussexes would have refused to disclose any of that: but they should have been asked – and been told that a vague denunciation remains just that without proof.

Oprah had the possibility of teasing out what was true and what was false in the couple's presentation of their "escape" from the palace, but made no attempt to do so.

The technique on the part of the couple has backfired, at least in Harry's home country.

Most Britons, especially the older ones, saw the interview as both self-pitying and self-aggrandising – the spectacle of two very wealthy and privileged individuals posing as victims to attract sympathy and greater fame.

William – who, if the way in which

The only way to know about such allegations is to know the details: the who, what, when, where and, if possible, why

the British head of state emerges remains as it currently is, will be king one day – seems to have fallen for the victimhood trap, with his own allegations that his mother's interview was corrupted by the means of obtaining it.

To be sure, Martin Bashir, then at the BBC, lied to her and to her brother to obtain the interview.

But William's assertion that she would have been less extreme had she not been encouraged by Bashir's claim that her staff and circle were plotting against her seems far-fetched.

Diana, when alive, provided ample evidence that she saw and conducted the interview as an opportunity to say what she wished about her husband's affair. In making the charge, William reduced rather than protected his mother, depriving her of agency to give her side of the story, which she was certainly entitled to do.

She had foreshadowed this in providing details for Andrew Morton's book, Diana: Her True Story, and in an interview with Max Hastings, then editor of The Daily Telegraph.

* * *

Celebrities, who command so much of the media space and are thus important components in our lives, should be interviewed.

In the nature of things, they will often be interviewed sycophantically since, especially for popular magazines, they are likely to increase circulation and thus have a power over the interviewer.

But the Oprah interview was on a different level. The Sussexes were not promoting a film or an event. They were promoting themselves.

They were there to justify their

decision to leave British royal duties for an independent life in the USA, and did so by alleging racism and meanness.

This put their interview squarely in the public domain and their contentions and claims were a matter for questioning and probing, as they would be for any others with power and status.

Oprah, with a huge reputation and a career which has seen her rise from poverty to great wealth and high status, has provided a malign example of how to deal with celebrities' allegations – specially of racism. That is, to put oneself on the side of the celebrity uncritically and to collaborate in the attempt to attract victim status, which is highly prized.

Meghan – with a mildly successful acting career behind her, with marriage into the wealthy Windsor family, with high-paying media and other opportunities opening up before her (at least for the moment), and with an $11m mansion in Montecito, California, and neighbours such as Tom Cruise, Ellen de Generes and Oprah herself in ➔

Buckingham Palace will investigate bullying allegations against Meghan

ABOVE: The Guardian newspaper on 4 March 2021, three days before the interview with Harry and Meghan premiered on television.

ABOVE: Prince Andrew during his interview with Emily Matlis, 2019

→ other mansions nearby – would seem to be an unlikely subject for sympathy or pity.

But a claim of racism, especially from a woman of colour, tends to silence all doubt and freeze all investigation.

It should not be if journalistic practice is to be observed.

Who asked the question about the baby's skin colour? Was it malicious or friendly? How did she react to it? How different was it from asking if the baby would have his father's red hair?

There are examples of proper interviews of princes and dukes: the best of which by some way was that to which Prince Andrew, the Queen's second son, submitted himself.

With an allegation hanging over him of having sex with a minor, arranged by convicted US sex trafficker Jeffrey Epstein – who killed himself in his prison cell in August 2019 – the prince

negotiated with the BBC Newsnight programme for an interview.

Finally, after some months of haggling, an interview conducted by presenter Emily Maitlis was set for November 2019.

The prince sought to distance himself from Epstein as much as possible, but Maitlis was remorseless, reminding him that he had visited his homes and his private island and flown in his private plane. Closing in, she asked if he had gone to stay after Epstein's release from jail in 2010 following a short sentence

for sexual assault of a minor.

When the prince framed his renewed contact with Epstein after his release as brief and for the purpose of drawing a line under the relationship, Maitlis reminded him he had gone to a celebratory dinner as guest of honour and had stayed in the New York mansion – a decision which the prince said had been "coloured by my tendency to be too honourable".

The core of the issue was the question: Did Andrew have sex with Virginia Roberts, then underage, in 2001, in London, at a house belonging to Ghislaine Maxwell, an associate of Epstein and now herself facing a delayed trial for sex trafficking?

The prince firmly and repeatedly denied any knowledge of Roberts, saying he had been with his daughter Beatrice at a party in a pizza restaurant in Windsor on the day Roberts had alleged the meeting.

He also denied later meetings, at which Roberts also alleged they had met and had sex. After some more exchanges, during which the prince spoke of the charity work he did, the interview ended.

But it was widely considered that Andrew had dug himself deeper into the hole he was already in.

Interviews have become markedly more probing over the past few decades. When Prince Charles gave an interview to Jonathan Dimbleby in June 1994, it was set within a generally upbeat documentary stressing his charity work and interests. Yet even here, and even though Dimbleby was a friend of the prince, Dimbleby asked Charles if he tried to be "faithful and honourable" to his wife.

 Diana, when alive, provided ample evidence that she saw and conducted the interview as an opportunity to say what she wished about her husband's affair

Hearing that he absolutely had tried, Dimbleby followed up with: "And you were?"

That elicited the response "Yes", with Charles adding – after a slight pause – "Until it became irretrievably broken down, us both having tried."

This response was a forerunner to his son Harry's response on receiving support from papa: that is, there would be no "contradiction" if "irretrievable breakdown" had set in quite soon after the marriage. Still, it did get some part of the truth into the public domain.

It was not a popular semi-truth. Even now, years later, Charles has a mediocre approval rating, coming in at number eight among the royals in a YouGov poll earlier this year. That is not good for one who is likely to be the next British monarch. In April, another poll showed a majority wanted William rather than Charles to succeed the Queen.

On the Queen's abdication or death, the monarchy will inevitably lose a great deal of its popularity. Who is to succeed her, how much the successor is likely to change the monarchy, how far a Charles III reign would be one in which the monarch intervenes much more actively in political issues than his mother did… all these are crucial areas of discussion and debate which should involve Charles, and others of the family, in interviews and analysis.

Whoever succeeds, he – it seems certain to be a man, though Princess Anne, at 70 and 16th in line to the throne, would probably be a safer pair of hands – will be titular head of a major state. Much of the job is ceremonial and display but, because the Queen conducts herself with scrupulous attention to neutrality in all matters, we have forgotten that a less disciplined monarch might see it as his right to intervene in policy issues. That has been Charles's habit and it calls for examination.

The Queen has provided something of a shield to her children's and grandchildren's faults. Without that,

When bad-mouthing the royals is a crime

BENJAMIN LYNCH writes about the countries where criticising rules is severely punished

LÈSE-MAJESTÉ IS A French term meaning "to do wrong to majesty" which, taken literally, could itself be a contentious point in law.

Heaven forbid anyone should question the majesty and spotless record of the UK's Prince Andrew, for instance.

But condemnation of the royal pizza connoisseur aside, the law – which covers general criticism of royalty – is a serious problem in many countries and has viciously targeted innocent individuals both historically and today.

The term can also refer to general laws regarding criticism of high-office public figures, but these are not always sanctioned specifically under lèse-majesté legislation.

In January, in Thailand, a woman in her 60s was given a cumulative sentence of 43 years in prison simply for sharing audio clips on social media that were critical of the Thai monarchy. The sentence was originally 87 years but was reduced due to a guilty plea. It followed a spate of arrests and convictions based on minor criticisms of King Maha Vajiralongkorn.

It is in Thailand where the most severe laws regarding this particular type of criticism exist, and this has been met by mass protests in recent years – primarily by students. Some 103 people currently face prosecution.

In Thailand, a woman was given a sentence of 43 years simply for sharing audio clips that were critical of the Thai monarchy.

Article 112 of the criminal code states violations are punishable by between three and 15 years in prison. Chillingly, it also grants anyone the power to file a complaint against a fellow citizen.

As exiled Thai monarchy critic Pavin Chachavalpongpun explained in a previous edition of Index: "As a result, use of the lèse-majesté law can come from all angles. An elder brother filed a complaint against his younger brother. A boss threated to take his employer to court."

Kuwait, Bahrain and Jordan all have their own version of the law and have particularly alarming records. Malaysia reneged on a moratorium of the 1948 Sedition Act as recently as 2018.

Not all lèse-majesté laws are historic relics of a more restrictive past. In 2018, an amendment in Cambodian law was made to give monetary fines or sentences of up to five years for anyone deemed to "defame, insult or threaten the king".

Saudi Arabia, where the ruling royal family were the instigators of the brutal killing of critic and journalist Jamal Khashoggi, does not have a formal legal code. Instead, its interpretation of sharia law dictates how criticism is punished, meaning denunciation of the royals is easily (and often brutally) clamped down on.

In the UK, there has not been a conviction under this rule since 1715, but various places in Europe still have such laws.

Monaco, Denmark, Belgium, Sweden and the Netherlands all have lèse-majesté laws. Although they are rarely (if ever) enforced, defamatory statements can, in theory, be more easily punished.

But Spain has continued to employ its draconian legislation. A number of rappers, most recently Pablo Hasél in February, have been sent to jail.

their characters would be more nakedly exposed.

Journalism has to be ready for that exposure: neither deferential nor celebrity interviews should feature in its coverage because the country's kings and queens still matter to its democracy. ✖

John Lloyd is a contributing editor at the Financial Times

50(03):86/89|DOI:10.1177/03064220211048876

A bulletin of frustration

It is the human stories that make us determined to be a voice for the persecuted, says **RUTH SMEETH**

WHEN STEPHEN SPENDER wrote in The Times on 15 October 1971 on the launch of Index on Censorship he warned that: "there is the risk of a magazine of this kind becoming a bulletin of frustration". He counselled that our publication should instead feature the best censored works making us not a grievance sheet but a bastion of hope.

Fifty years later, I regularly reflect on his words to remind myself that behind every heart-breaking story, behind every headline there is a person and a family that we are striving to support. That by shining a spotlight on their plight we are offering hope and that by commissioning those who are being censored by repressive regimes we are not just demonstrating our solidarity, but we are also providing a voice for the persecuted. I know that I must hold onto his words otherwise the news from Afghanistan, Hong Kong, Belarus and Myanmar over the summer would have broken me.

Many of us would have been moved to tears by the news in recent weeks. I am not sure I have ever felt more impotent than when I went to meet my local Afghani community, who were desperate for news of their families who are living in fear of Taliban reprisals. Their stories of women fleeing Taliban raids, of brothers who are in hiding, of parents who they can no longer get money to for food.

One of the men I met was truly desperate. His wife and four-month-old daughter are trapped in Kabul and he cannot get them out. When we met he was looking how to return to Afghanistan to be with them to protect them, knowing that he could be murdered on his he return. Being in the UK knowing that they were targets because of him was destroying him.

These are the stories behind the headlines. And they, like so many examples of the pages of this magazine, wish to be heard, want the world to know their stories, their struggles and their determination. These people, each one of them an inspiration, drive each one of us to be better, to want to do more, to try and help. Which is why Index on Censorship really exists, to bring hope – to demonstrate real solidarity and to make it clear, in as public a way as we can, that these people are not alone. That someone is listening, that someone cares.

And it is in this tradition that we have launched a new programme of work on the pages of the magazine today. This, our Climate of Fear special edition, is published in the days leading up to the COP26 global summit, a conference bringing together the leaders of nearly every nation state in an effort to halt the impact of climate change. It is all too easy for the debate on climate change to focus on the economic impact, on the geo-politics or on the global challenges we face. But the reality is that climate change and environmental disasters have a very human cost. The families that are forced to move, the drinking water that becomes unsafe, the crops that fail.

We assume that there is always a legal redress for these communities, but in too many cases the people fighting for justice are unable to access legal systems that are fit for purpose. Too many tyrants are dismissive of the challenges of climate change and are on the side of the polluters rather than their people. Which is why we're delighted to be able to launch a new work programme, supported by the Clifford Chance Foundation. This project seeks to empower those who are working on environmental issues globally, by giving them a voice. It will provide a platform for these activists to share the struggles they are facing as a result of their work, including coordinated efforts to censor them. We will continue to cover this ahead of COP26 and beyond.

Climate change affects all of us, but the impact is not equal. Some of the most vulnerable in our global community bear the brunt of environmental failures. Indigenous people throughout the world are facing increasing obstacles to challenge the impact on their communities.

It is these people who need their stories told and Index will be a platform for them. We will also, with the support of the Clifford Chance Foundation, be publishing our first Index in over a decade, highlighting the regimes which are the worst offenders in efforts to restrict free expression related to environmental impact. This is a crucially important project and one that should have lasting impact and provide an evidence base to challenge those who seek to deny climate change. ✖

Ruth Smeeth is chief executive of Index on Censorship

> Too many tyrants are dismissive of the challenges of climate change and are on the side of the polluters

50(03):90/90|DOI:10.1177/03064220211048877

CULTURE

On being told by Fox News host Bill O'Reilly that he was a "dangerous man", Baraka responded: "You're more dangerous – you have a TV show"

DAVID GRUNDY LOOKS AT THE LEGACY OF CONTROVERSIAL POET AMIRI BARAKA | THE MAN WHO BLEW UP AMERICA P92

The man who blew up America

DAVID GRUNDY looks at the legacy of controversial poet **AMIRI BARAKA**

POET, PLAYWRIGHT, ACTIVIST and critic Amiri Baraka (LeRoi Jones) remains a controversial figure seven years after his death.

Too often, however, his career is viewed through a series of sensationalist snapshots and out-of-context statements, reducing the history of US white supremacy to a mere background blur.

One of the architects of the Black Arts Movement that swept the USA, articulating a new sense of artistic and political self-determination, Baraka was a frequent target of state authorities.

William J Maxwell's book, FB Eyes, provides detailed accounts of how FBI agents surveilled African-American writers through this period, acting as judges, censors, spies and de facto literary critics.

After years of such treatment, poet Ray Durem – a former member of the International Brigades later associated with the Umbra group – wrote the sarcastic epistle A Gold Watch To The FBI Man Who Has Followed Me For 25 Years.

In 1953, Paul Robeson presented to a petition to the UN entitled We Charge Genocide.

In the 1960s, as attempts were made

to enlist black culture for the Cultural Cold War – state-sponsored tours by jazz musicians, CIA-fronted magazines – segregation, racial terrorism and underdevelopment continued.

Baraka's grandfather had been driven from town having run for political office in Dothan, Alabama, and racial violence was never far from Baraka's mind.

Growing up in Newark, New Jersey – a city with a large black population ruled by white politicians and plagued by mafia corruption – Baraka studied at Howard University before joining the air force ("error farce"), self-educating in texts from Finnegans Wake to The Communist Manifesto.

Relocating to New York, he befriended poets Allen Ginsberg and Frank O'Hara, publishing the magazines Yūgen – with his first wife, Hettie – and The Floating Bear, with poet Diane di Prima.

Through the latter, he had his first major encounter with censorship.

In June 1961, The Floating Bear's ninth issue published William Burroughs's story Roosevelt After the Inauguration, a scatological attack in which Roosevelt appoints a baboon to the Supreme Court.

One of its subscribers happened to be a prison inmate, and prison censors reported the newsletter for obscenity to US postal authorities.

Baraka defended himself in court, "read[ing] all the good parts of Ulysses and Catullus aloud to the jury".

The Floating Bear announced his acquittal with a quote from boxer Joe Louis: "Hello Ma, I Glad I Win!"

The case formed part of a rising tide challenging the repressive atmosphere of McCarthyism. Writers such as Burroughs, Ginsberg, O'Hara and John

Wieners were publishing explicit queer texts at a time when homosexual acts were illegal, combining the traditions of the American left with radically open new modes of expression.

From 1962 to 1965, Ed Sanders ran Fuck You: A Magazine of the Arts "Dedicated to Pacifism, Unilateral Disarmament, National Defence thru Nonviolent Resistance, Multilateral Indiscriminate Apertural Conjugation, Anarchism, World Federalism, Civil Disobedience, Obstructers & Submarine Boarders, And All Those Groped by J Edgar Hoover in the Silent Halls of Congress", publishing Burroughs, Baraka and sexually explicit poets including Wieners and Lenore Kandel. Unsurprisingly, the authorities raided his Peace Eye Bookstore.

GINSBERG WAS PROSECUTED but acquitted at the Howl trial of 1957; Burroughs's Naked Lunch was banned in Boston from 1962 to 1966p; and a 1964 production of Baraka's play The Eighth Ditch was shut down by the NYPD.

Alongside these generally white writers, Baraka encountered the experimental and politically militant black poets of the Umbra Workshop, many of whom he met at the UN Building in New York in 1961 while protesting the assassination of Patrice Lumumba, the prime minister of the Republic of the Congo.

Umbra members, involved in the campaign for exiled self-defence advocate Robert F Williams and his comrade Mae Mallory, were themselves subject to police harassment.

Later, Umbra member Lennox Raphael was embroiled in a censorship case concerning on-stage nudity in his play Che!

Baraka's own reputation as a poet and jazz critic, and his Obie Award-winning play Dutchman (1964), drew him further into the public eye. He was poised to become the token black writer admitted to the literary establishment every generation "as if", he remarked,

"the door to the American Dream had just swung open".

Instead, he moved to Harlem, spearheading the Black Arts Repertory Theatre/School (BART/S). Partially funded with government "war on poverty" money, BART/S sponsored Black Nationalist readings, concerts and classes, calling for the overthrow of the government.

Baraka's essay The Revolutionary Theatre was commissioned but turned down by The New York Times. Published instead in the anti-imperialist magazine Liberator, it proclaimed: "This is a theatre of assault. The play that will split the heavens for us will be called The Destruction of America."

Baraka anticipated the response, saying: "American cops will try to close the theatres where such nakedness of the human spirit is paraded."

Sure enough, the authorities closed BART/S down. Baraka left New York as LeRoi Jones and emerged in Newark as Amiri Baraka – Swahili-ised Arabic meaning "blessed prince".

In 1967, rumours spread that Newark police had shot dead yet another unarmed black citizen. In the subsequent unrest, Baraka drove around picking up injured people   ➔

> Baraka forced the question of what it means when the freedom of speech of some is enshrined without thought, while others are continually silenced.

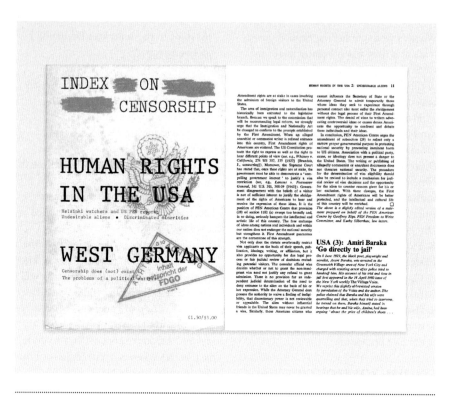

ABOVE: The 5/1980 issue of Index on Censorship, the only one in which Baraka was published.

→ from the street, and was himself arrested, accused of weapons possession, jailed, beaten and put on trial. When a notoriously racist judge read out to the (white) jury Baraka's poem Black People!, recently published in the Evergreen Review, substituting the swearwords with the word "blank", Baraka pointed out the absurdity, as if he were on trial for a poem.

With supporting statements from old friends including Ginsberg and from Jean-Paul Sartre, he was acquitted.

Now a national political figure, Baraka drove Kenneth Gibson's successful campaign to become Newark's first black mayor. But Gibson turned back on his promises, and by the mid-1970s Baraka, under the influence of African revolutionaries such as Tanzanian exile Abdulrahman Mohamed Babu and "Black Bolshevik" Harry Haywood, moved to Pan-African socialism and then to communism.

His reputation with publishers soon soured. Putnam's had commissioned a

novel with a huge advance, expecting a black Godfather. Instead, they got Baraka's political roman-a-clef, Six Persons, which remained unpublished for decades.

For several years, publishers wouldn't touch his play The Sidney Poet Heroical for fear of libel trials. They were likewise wary of poems with titles such as Rockefeller is Yo Vice President, and Yo Mamma Don't Wear No Drawers; Stop Killer Cops; and The Dictatorship of the Proletariat. There were also lines such as "We'll worship Jesus/ When Jesus do / Somethin / When Jesus blow up / the white house / or blast nixon down".

Meanwhile, Baraka warned of the USA's rightward turn in his 1976 play S-1, concerning "a repressive Senate Bill that would negate several of the Bill of Rights".

In 1979, police intervened in an argument between Baraka and his wife, the poet Amina. Witnesses were intimidated, a knife was planted, Baraka was sent to jail.

HIS ARTICLE ON the incident marks the only time he appeared in Index on Censorship. An editorial note points out that even if there may be "difficulty in identifying prisoners of conscience in a country [the USA] where there is no overt political imprisonment [...] it is suspected that many people may be 'framed' on criminal charges because of their political activity or ethnic origin".

Baraka's article described the "ghetto-jailhouse wipeout syndrome" – what Angela Davis would later name the "prison-industrial complex" – as "a turnstile spinning [people of colour] in and out of the slam with a relentless mindlessness".

Sentenced to 48 consecutive weekends in a halfway house, Baraka wrote his autobiography and, following his release, continued to do cultural and political work in Newark.

He ran poetry and music sessions in his basement, attended by the great and the good of Newark's thriving jazz scene.

A respected figure and elder statesman, he spoke at James Baldwin's funeral alongside Toni Morrison and Maya Angelou: his influence and standing were undeniable, even as he continued to be neglected due to his politics.

Baraka wrote the poem Somebody Blew Up America in October 2001, against the build-up to the "war on terror": indiscriminate attacks on people of colour, and the rhetorical drumbeating of Fox News and the administration of president George W Bush.

When he read the poem in 2002, after his appointment as Poet Laureate of New Jersey, the case hit national headlines.

Governor Jim McGreevey demanded his apology and resignation. Baraka refused, invoking the right to free speech. Unable to force him to quit, the state abolished the post.

Critiques of the poem were often tone-deaf, ignoring its formal and historical context. By contrast, Anthony Olszewski points out the poem's systematic détournement of Vachel Lindsay's racist poem The Congo

– for many years taught in literature departments without the blink of an eye.

Unleashing a catalogue of "the various forces of terror Afro-Americans and other oppressed people of the world have suffered: slavery, colonialism, imperialism, neo-colonialism, national oppression", Baraka asks – to paraphrase – "who, both historically and in the continuing epoch of racial capitalism, are the real terrorists?"

He's spot-on when he asks, "Who made Bush president / Who believe the confederate flag need to be flying", or when he invokes the genocide of Native Americans, the persecution of US leftists (many of them Jewish), the Holocaust, the Atlantic slave trade and the afterlife of slavery.

Unfortunately, four lines pick up on 9/11 conspiracy theories suggesting an inside job of which the Israeli government had advance notice. Baraka stood by this passage, but few writers can be considered ideologically error-free, whether they admit it or not.

And whereas white writers – particularly white male writers – from Pound to Updike are let off the hook, writers of colour such as Baraka are singled out.

Schools and states across America have censored texts by black writers from Richard Wright to Alice Childress. And despite the marketing uptick of black culture following the George Floyd rebellion last year, black culture is still routinely ignored or denounced by white commentators.

Baraka's earlier work of the 1960s contains misogynist, antisemitic and homophobic statements.

He was the first to admit this, and was sometimes his own harshest critic, as his essay Confessions of a Former Anti-Semite and autobiography reveal.

Criticised for misogyny and homophobia by black activists such as Angela Davis and Cheryl Clarke, Baraka listened and changed.

Both Baraka's sister, Kimako, in the 1980s, and his daughter Shani,

in the early 2000s, were murdered in homophobic attacks.

In a moving open letter, he condemned "not only the actual ignorant negro, homophobic, male-chauvinist, black-woman-hating murderer, as a person, but as an idea, a philosophy, an ideology, roaming though so many minds".

Baraka's writing is undeniably and deliberately abrasive. It had to be.

So too is the work of June Jordan, Audre Lorde, Jayne Cortez, Sonia Sanchez and Nikki Giovanni. Jordan's Poem About Police Violence asks:

Tell me something
what you think would happen
if everytime they kill a black boy
then we kill a cop
everytime they kill a black man
then we kill a cop
you think the accident rate would
lower subsequently?

It's a rhetorical question, and an unanswerable one: unanswerable, that is, within discourse that explains away the daily violence undergirding racial capitalism.

For several years, publishers wouldn't touch his play The Sidney Poet Heroical for fear of libel trials. They were likewise wary of poems with titles such as Rockefeller is Yo Vice President

By reversing the rhetoric that enables killer-cops, vigilantes and domestic abusers to walk free, Jordan forces a conversation.

Readers may react with horror to the idea of revenge killing, but what of the horror at the fact that such murders happen in the first place?

Focusing on the rhetorical violence of Black Arts Movement writing – say, a poem's imagined influence on "rioters" (itself a racist stereotype) as invoked in Baraka's 1967 trial – lets white supremacy off the hook.

On being told by Fox News host Bill O'Reilly that he was a "dangerous man", Baraka responded: "You're more dangerous – you have a TV show."

Throughout his life, Baraka forced the question of what it means when the freedom of speech of some is enshrined without thought, while others are continually silenced.

He spoke out against the silencing of dissidents from South Africa to South Korea, and against the continuing legacy of imperialism, Dixie and the KKK. The latest specimen of this was Donald Trump, whose presidency he didn't live to see but about which he would not have been surprised.

One of his last poems, What's That Who Is This In Them Old Nazi Clothes? Nazi's Dead, ends:

This new anti-fascist war we must
fight, against the rule of
The corpses. The corporate
dictatorship forming in front of
Our eyes. It can no longer
surprise. Get your pitch forks
ready.
Strike Hard and True. You get
them or they get you.

We ignore Baraka's legacy at our peril. ✖

David Grundy is a poet whose works include Relief Efforts and To The Reader.

50(03):92/95|DOI:10.1177/03064220211048878

Suffering in silence

BENJAMIN LYNCH looks at the work of Afghan poet **PARWANA FAYYAZ**, celebrating the women of her homeland

DOCUMENTING THE LIVES of women in Afghanistan, Forty Names by Afghan poet Parwana Fayyaz is a poignant reminder of lost opportunities, of freedoms given and then taken away, of a new generation living without enlightenment through education.

The collection, the title verse of which won the 2019 Forward Prize for Best Single Poem "focusses on stories and experiences from my childhood" and the ingrained attitude of acceptance that comes with a lack of schooling.

The title itself is reference to one of those very stories, where 40 women throw themselves off a cliff in order to protect their honour, rather than die with dishonour.

As she told Carcanet Press: "I grew up among women who told stories, stories concerning women. As the time passed, the women themselves became the stories. The majority of these women never went to school. They share their philosophy of life down through generations. [They say] "in the face of hardship, be patient, patience is the remedy"."

Born in 1990, Fayyaz's education challenges this idea. Now with a PhD in Persian Studies from Cambridge University, how can silence possibly make sense?

To suffer in silence is seen as a token of patience

"When I left my home and Afghanistan to embark on my journey to become more educated, I began to reflect on the lives of the women I had always admired," she said. "I began to question my admiration for them. They were suffering and yet they accepted it. To suffer in silence is seen as a token of patience."

"With more education, patience became more elusive."

Indeed, the choice now for so many women and girls in Afghanistan, sadly, is only silence and patience, but without the reward the piety is supposed to bring. As the Taliban tightens its stranglehold over the country, it forces out the oxygen required for art and literature to flourish and for women to learn how to express themselves in this sense.

Certainly, more than they previously should have done, everyday people in the west are taking notice of Afghanistan. The stories and images that have shocked so many people are not new, but it quite obviously takes a feeling of personal involvement – Nato troops were caught in a dangerous evacuation process – for people to take notice for long.

Even the process of translation for Fayyaz was important in this regard, "My poetry makes use of the art of translation to enhance the meaning of my story-poems for a Western audience, specifically involving the translation of Persian names into English. In active translation, the Persian names are the sounds and the English translations their echoes."

Perhaps, to the English-speaking world, the plight of Afghans under the Taliban will remain as far-distant noises that will not reverberate so loudly for long. Forty Names, then, is in its truest sense a reflection of what has been lost for a whole generation of Afghan girls: a reminder that Afghanistan's brief experience of democracy will never be forgotten. ✖

Forty Names was published in July 2021 by Carcanet Press, carcanet.co.uk

50(03):96/99|DOI:10.1177/03064220211048879

Forty Names

I
Zib was young.
Her youth was all she cared for.
These mountains were her cots
the wind her wings, and those pebbles were her friends.
Their clay hut, a hut for all the eight women,
and her Father, a shepherd.

He knew every cave and all possible ponds.
He took her to herd with him,
as the youngest daughter
Zib marched with her father.
She learnt the ways to the caves and the ponds.

Young women gathered there for water, the young
girls with the bright dresses, their green
eyes were the muses.

Behind those mountains
she dug a deep hole,
storing a pile of pebbles.

II
The daffodils
never grew here before,
but what is this yellow sea up high on the hills?

A line of some blue wildflowers.
In a lane toward the pile of tumbleweeds
all the houses for the cicadas,
all your neighbors.
And the eagle roars in the distance,
have you met them yet?

The sky above, through the opaque skin of
your dust, carries whims from the mountains,
it brings me a story.
The story of forty young bodies.

III
A knock,
father opened the door.

There stood the fathers,
the mothers' faces startled.
All the daughters standing behind them.
In the pit of dark night,
their yellow and turquoise colors
lining the sky.

'Zibon, my daughter,
take them to the cave.'
She was handed a lantern;
she took the way.
Behind her a herd of colors flowing.
The night was slow,
the sound of their footsteps a solo music of a mystic.

Names:
Sediqa, Hakima, Roqia,
Firoza, Lilia, Soghra.
Shah Bakhat, Shah Dokht, Zamaroot,
Naznin, Gul Badan, Fatima, Fariba.
Sharifa, Marifa, Zinab, Fakhria, Shahparak, MahGol,
Latifa, Shukria, Khadija, Taj Begum, Kubra, Yaqoot,
Nadia, Zahra, Shima, Khadija, Farkhunda, Halima, Mahrokh, Nigina,
Maryam, Zarin, Zara, Zari, Zamin,
Zarina,

at last Zibon.

IV
No news. Neither drums nor flutes of
shepherds reached them, they
remained in the cave. Were
people gone?

Once in every night, an exhausting
tear dropped – heard from someone's mouth,
a whim. A total silence again.

Zib calmed them.
Each daughter
crawled under her veil,
slowly the last throbs from the mill-house
also died.
No throbbing. No pond. No nights.
Silence became an exhausting noise.

➔

→
V
Zib led the daughters to the mountains.

The view of the thrashing horses, the brown uniforms
all puzzled them. Imagined
the men snatching their skirts, they feared.

We will all meet in paradise,
with our honored faces
angels will greet us.

A wave of colors dived behind the mountains,
freedom was sought in their veils, their colors
flew with wind. Their bodies freed and slowly hit

the mountains. One by one, they rested. Women
figures covered the other side of the mountains.
Hairs tugged. Heads stilled. Their arms curved
beside their twisted legs.

These mountains became their cots.
The wind their wings, and those pebbles their friends.
Their rocky cave, a cave for all the forty women.
And their fathers and mothers disappeared.

Three Dolls

During the wars,
my mother made our clothes
and our toys.

For her three daughters,
she made dresses, and once
she made us each a doll.

Their figures were made with sticks
gathered from our neighbor's garden.
She rolled white cotton fabric
around the stick frames
to create a skin for each doll.

Then she fattened the skin
with cotton extracted from an old pillow.
With black and red yarns bought from
uncle Farid's store, my mother created faces.
A unique face for each doll.

Large black eyes, thick eyelashes and eyebrows.
Long black hair, a smudge of black for each nose.
And lips in red.
Our dolls came alive,
with each stitch of my mother's sewing needle.

We dyed their cheeks with red rose-petals,
and fashioned skirts from bits of fabric,
from my mother's sewing basket.
And finally, we named our dolls.

Mine with a skirt of royal green was the oldest and tallest,
and I called her Duur. Pearl.
Shabnam chose a skirt of bright yellow
and called her doll, Pari. Angel.
And our youngest sister, Gohar, chose deep blue fabric,
and named her doll, Raang. Color.

They lived longer than our childhoods.

Her Name is Flower Sap

Somewhere – in the no-man's land,
there are high mountains, and there is a woman.

The mountains are seemingly unreachable.
The woman in her anonymity is untraceable.

The mountains are called the Tora Bora.
The woman is known as Sharbet Gula, Flower Sap.

In her faded-ruby-red Chador, she appeared
a young girl with a frown, with her green eyes.

Not knowing where to look.
When the world looked back at her.

As young kids, refugees of wartime in Pakistan
we were equally intrigued with her photograph.

'Her eyes have the magic of good and bad.'
'The light of her eyes can destroy fighter jets.'

So went Afghan children's conversation
in the aftermath of 9/11. 'But could she take down

The Taliban jets,' we wondered,
as the jets crossed the skies in one song.

But Flower Sap could never answer us.
For she had disappeared like our childhood.

*

As the borders became damper lands,
Afghans like soft worms crawled toward their homeland.

In the in-between mountains,
Flower Sap re-appeared, without any answers.

Now she was a grown-up woman.
A mother of four girls. A widow.

There were some questions in her eyes.
The ones I had seen in my parents' eyes.

Where do we go next? Now that our country is free.
She still did not have any answers.

And where was the power of her eyes?
I then saw her smiling. As an immigrant, I smiled too.

For her name saved the day.
She was taken to a hospital for her eyes.

The president of the county met her,
and sent her on a pilgrimage.

Her name educated her daughters,
it gave her a house and a reason to return to her homeland.

What else is there in the names and naming?
If not for reparation. ✖

Heart and sole

MARK FRARY shares an exclusive extract from a new translation by Peirene Press that chronicles author **KATJA OSKAMP'S** retraining as a chiropodist and the colourful lives of her clients in former East Germany

WHEN MID-LIFE CRISIS hits, some have affairs, others buy powerful motorbikes. Not Katja Oskamp. When the Leipzig-born playwright hit the middle years, Oskamp retrained to become a chiropodist.

She writes in the introduction to her new book Marzahn, Mon Amour that "the middle years, when you're neither young nor old, are fuzzy years. You can no longer see the shore you started from, but you can't yet get a clear enough view of the shore you're heading for. You spend these years thrashing about in the middle of a big lake, out of breath, flagging from the tedium of swimming."

Her life had become stale and her writing "a little iffy", she says.

The problems people had with their feet became her salvation and, in the process, reinvigorated her writing.

After a course in chiropody that saw her confuse claw and hammer toes, cuticle nippers and nail clippers and learn the 26 bones in the foot, she started caring for peoples' feet in the Berlin district of Marzahn which, as part of East Germany, was turned from a rural district into a series of vast, towering housing estates.

"At first, I didn't tell anyone about my decision to retrain," writes Oskamp.

"But afterwards, when I was swanning around with my certificate, I came up against revulsion, incomprehension and, the hardest to bear, sympathy. From writer to chiropodist – what a spectacular comedown."

But starting at the bottom has returned her to the top. Her book Marzahn, Mon Amour brilliantly weaves together the foot problems of the built-up suburb's residents with fabulously gossipy stories of their lives both pre- and post- the fall of the Berlin Wall. When published in its original German, it became an overnight sensation thanks to its stories of corns, ingrown toenails and fungal infections.

Maddie Rogers of publisher Peirene Press says, "Once the largest prefabricated housing estate in the GDR, Marzahn is now home to a multitude of pensioners in need of foot care. From her intimate vantage point, the chiropodist keenly observes the clients who pass through her clinic and recounts their life stories with poignancy and humour. Each story stands alone as a beautifully crafted vignette; together they form a nuanced and tender portrait of a community. Part memoir, part collective history, this is Katja Oskamp's love letter to the inhabitants of Marzahn."

Peirene Press was founded in 2008 by Meike Ziervogel with the purpose of bringing more European literature onto the UK scene, where translated literature makes up only a tiny percentage of books published. It has published works in translation from 17 different languages, with a focus on contemporary literature and short novels and offers a subscription service where subscribers receive books two months ahead of publication.

The literature published by Peirene encompasses both social and political issues. Between 2016 and 2018 it produced the Peirene Now! series, a collection of commissioned works exploring contemporary issues such as Brexit and the refugee crisis. This series included Shatila Stories, a piece of collaborative fiction written by nine Syrian and Palestinian refugees.

It has also published Shadows on the Tundra, the memoir of Lithuanian Dalia Grinkevičiūtė who was deported to a Soviet labour camp at the age of 14 in 1941; Under the Tripoli Sky by Kamal Ben Hameda, a glimpse into deeply segregated pre-Gaddafi Libyan society; and Soviet Milk by Latvian author Nora Ikstena, which examines the effects of Soviet rule on one individual's life.

The following extract is taken from Marzahn, Mon Amour, translated from German by Jo Heinrich, out in February 2022 (subscribers receive it in December 2021, **peirenepress.com**). ✖

Mark Frary is associate editor at Index on Censorship

> The middle years, when you're neither young nor old, are fuzzy years. You can no longer see the shore you started from, but you can't yet get a clear enough view of the shore you're heading for.

50(03):100/103|DOI: 10.1177/03064220211048880

Herr Pietsch

By Katja Oskamp
Translated from the German by Jo Heinrich

MANY PEOPLE THINK Marzahn is teeming with former GDR bigwigs and SED party officials. It's not true; I'd stake my life on it, especially as I work here. I look after the feet of former bricklayers, butchers and nurses. There's also a woman who worked in electronics, one who bred cattle and another who was a petrol pump attendant.

There is, though, one dyed-in-the-wool party functionary who visits me regularly. Since I've known him, the stereotype has acquired a name: Herr Pietsch. He is a walking cliché.

Herr Pietsch arrives promptly at the salon door for his appointments, checked flat cap on his bald head, peering imperiously through the window. It is beneath him to knock on a door or ring a bell; a door needs to be opened on Herr Pietsch's arrival. That's what he knows and expects, even if it hasn't been that way for thirty years. I let him in with a 'Greetings, Herr Pietsch', but my smile is not returned. Herr Pietsch silently hangs up his jacket, giving the impression that he's here on official business, to make some kind of inspection. He acknowledges a woman waiting in the wicker chair for her beauty treatment, looking down on her in every sense, given his height. He leads me into the chiropody room, taking his little bag with him.

'How are things with you?' I ask.

Herr Pietsch, taking off his shoes and socks, stares out of the window. By now I know the routine: he is always wary at first, only to drastically overstep the mark later. I bend down, push the footbath into place and look up into his protruding eyes – two bulging orbs. Herr Pietsch speaks with a Thuringian-Saxon accent, a little indistinctly as he's on his third set of teeth: 'There are certainly a few things I'm not happy with, but I'm getting by. I'm on top of life.'

Eberhard Pietsch was born in 1941 into a modest family. He attended a Workers' and Peasants' College, and became a teacher of history and mathematics. He got married and had a daughter. He soon changed tack professionally and started his career as a party official. At first, he ran a branch of the Free German Youth in Thuringia, but before long he was promoted to a party position. He once boasted to me, 'I was the youngest district party secretary in the whole of the GDR!' The district whose party secretary he had been in the 70s bordered West Germany and I was given the impression that Herr Pietsch had guarded all twenty-one miles of the frontier by himself. In 1981 Herr Pietsch moved to the capital with his family, went to conferences in other socialist countries as an SED official, and accompanied GDR delegations to the Olympic Games. I've never found out exactly what his job entailed.

When he first came to see me, he asked me if I knew when the Pioneers' Anniversary was. 'Thirteenth of December,' I said, and then, on request, recited the dates of National People's Army Day (1 March), Teacher's Day (12 June) and Republic Day (7 October), and I even sang 'May There Always Be Sunshine' in Russian for him, as a little extra. This won me a place in his faltering heart. In me, he sees the diligent young Pioneer I once was. I remind Herr Pietsch of his prime.

While I'm washing his feet, he tells me about a new armchair he's bought. He'll have to wait three months for it to be delivered. As he's already got rid of his old armchair, a camping chair is all he has to sit on for now. I dry his long feet, which hang from long legs, reminding me of a hare's paws. Then I step on the pedal, sending Herr Pietsch skywards with a low hum.

In his prime, Herr Pietsch found himself not only politically and ideologically on the right side, but also on the high ground, to his mind at least. He was a cut above, with others below. It's a concept that, deep down, Herr Pietsch has held on to. As I'm familiar with the special dates and songs, I find myself on the right side in Herr Pietsch's eyes, even if I am just a lowly chiropodist. In his prime, as an influential man, Herr Pietsch didn't just go away on business, he often played away too: here an ambitious ➔

ABOVE: Housing estate in Berlin-Marzahn

I get the better of his woody toenails, which are never easy to trim. I run a probe under the edges of his nails. It triggers his nerve endings, making Herr Pietsch's toes twitch every so often. He finds it unpleasant and maintains he has no control over it. The drill starts up with a buzz. I carefully even out the grooves in his nails and try to give the freshly trimmed edges a smooth shape, with only partial success given the brittle material I'm working with.

Herr Pietsch had just begun an affair with a buxom party colleague fourteen years his junior when the truth came out. His wife caught him in the act, washed her hands of him and threw him out of the marital home. At the time, not only Herr Pietsch's honour, but also the GDR was on its last legs. The Wall came down, East Germany was no more and Frau Pietsch got her divorce. While all of Berlin celebrated German reunification at the Brandenburg Gate, Herr Pietsch was moving into a one-room apartment in Marzahn, where he still lives (and currently sits on his camping chair). He wanted to get back into teaching, but he was turned down. To avoid unemployment, he started working for an insurance company in an office in Marzahn. He managed a customer base that had been absorbed from the GDR's state insurance scheme. After thirteen years of insurance, Herr Pietsch collapsed in the street. An ambulance. Heart surgery. Five bypasses in eight hours. After rehab, Herr Pietsch retired at sixty-three, on a very much pared-down pension.

While I'm scrubbing the rough skin from Herr Pietsch's withered feet, he talks about his next (and forty-third) hike with his cardiac rehab group, in which he takes a leading role. Herr Pietsch plans the hikes: he walks them in advance, times them, tests out the train connections and, once he has counted the names on the list he's passed round, books a table at an inn so the group can refuel and revive themselves at the end of their hike. If it's someone's birthday, Herr Pietsch prepares a speech to give to the group.

I interject to say that the cardiac rehab group must be happy that Herr Pietsch always organizes these hikes to perfection. Unexpectedly, Herr

→ comrade, there an interpreter or a track and field athlete. He had a long-term relationship with his secretary. Herr Pietsch must have kept meticulous records about these affairs, as he once told me the exact number of sexual conquests he'd had in his lifetime (fifty-one), on which I congratulated him, as would be expected of a chiropodist as far as Eberhard Pietsch is concerned.

Pietsch isn't pleased with my compliment, raising his brows over his goitrous eyes dismissively and retorting in his broad Saxony accent, 'Bassema off Mädschn' – in other words, 'Look here, young lady!' This kicks off an explanation that goes right back to basics, a wily fox telling a mentally underdeveloped creature that he can plan these hikes at the drop of a hat, thanks to his years of experience as a district party secretary. Herr Pietsch spells it out for me, almost as if I should be taking notes: 'I, Eberhard Pietsch, have always been able to organize anything! I, Eberhard Pietsch, know what the cardiac rehab group needs! I, Eberhard Pietsch, am good at public speaking!' Herr Pietsch has been living alone for almost thirty years. His relationship with his ex-wife is chilly and even his daughter keeps contact to a minimum.

Herr Pietsch isn't invited round for family birthdays. No one rings up every once in a while to find out how he is. Herr Pietsch signed over his garden plot to his grandson. The grandson took it on without a word of thanks and still never calls.

I rub the dust from Herr Pietsch's feet and reach for the cream. His skin absorbs it like a sponge and I need to top it up several times. Herr Pietsch starts on his illnesses and doesn't register his foot massage at all. He's lost contact not only with his relatives, but also with his feet. I could be poking in his ears, for all the notice he takes.

He talks of the cardiologist, the orthopaedist, the ophthalmologist and the dermatologist, and finally reaches the urologist, whom he visits intermittently for monitoring purposes. Her routine question about his sexual activity forms the transition to Herr Pietsch's central theme: erections, or, more specifically, his erections, which he goes on to describe in detail as attainable, although unreliable. Like the GDR, like his marriage and like his career, Herr Pietsch's erections are leaning towards a sudden collapse. He worries about the medication he's taking for his heart, but nevertheless wants to try out the tablets the urologist recommends for keeping it up. There's just one thing missing: a sexual partner. No sign of one, for miles. Then Herr Pietsch asks me if I might be interested in having sex with him. I tell him I'm already taken; he'll have to make do with a pedicure. But Herr Pietsch sticks to his guns. He says that I'm not stupid and that I have an 'erudite' air about me. I politely turn him down again. Despite, or maybe because of, his defeat, Herr Pietsch straightens himself up and says rather contritely that we'll move on from that subject now. Of course – he still needs to give the orders.

I put his socks back on, unroll his trouser legs, bring the chiropody chair down to ground level and pass Herr Pietsch the shoehorn. His hare's paws disappear into his shoes.

His meagre pension doesn't allow for any extravagance. He's labelled some envelopes that he keeps in his one-room apartment. He puts money aside in them for bigger expenses: the new armchair, a short trip back to his hometown in Thuringia and, last year, an International Garden Exhibition membership. One of his envelopes is for chiropody. Herr Pietsch first came every six weeks, then every five. Now he stands at the door every four weeks.

As I go to leave the room, with the now cold footbath in my hands, Herr Pietsch whips a mini bottle of Söhnlein Brillant sparkling wine out of his bag and presents me with it: 'Good work, Comrade.' I laugh and thank him for the present. Herr Pietsch puts his arm round my waist. 'Can I have a photo of you?'

'No,' I say, 'no photos, Herr Pietsch.'

His goitrous eyes look sad.

At the till, he tells me off – 'Look here, young lady' – as if I were his incompetent secretary: it can't be that difficult to find a new appointment; I must hurry up, he's got other things he needs to do today. I write the appointment in the diary and on Herr Pietsch's client card, put twenty-two euros in the till, lead him to the door and hold it open. He takes his leave seriously and professionally. The six-foot-three pensioner creeps off, checked flat cap on his bald head, back bent, empty bag in his hand. Oh, Eberhard, you old child of the workers and peasants. All your life, you've mistaken your position for your personality. Give my regards to the cardiac rehab group. ✖

Secret agenda

A reform of the UK's Official Secrets Act will have a significant chilling effect on journalists and investigative journalism. **MARTIN BRIGHT** reports

T IS NOW more than 20 years since The Guardian and The Observer fought off attempts by the UK government to force them to hand over documents in the case of MI5 whistleblower David Shayler. At a judicial review, Judge Igor Judge concluded that demands to hand over journalistic material "would have a devastating and stifling effect on the proper investigation of the ... story".

The case reinforced the special status of journalistic sources in law – even in official secrecy cases.

As the journalist who wrote about Shayler's disclosures, I am particularly concerned about proposals for reforming the Official Secrets Act.

These include enhanced search powers to give police access to just the sort of journalistic "special procedure material" (notes, emails and recorded interviews) we fought so hard to keep from the police two decades ago. The new OSA would thus enshrine in law the "devastating and stifling effect" on journalism that so concerned Judge.

Much has happened since The Guardian and The Observer's principled stand in the High Court: the growth of digital technology, the emergence of global Islamist terrorism and the increased national security threat from Russia and China have given the government good arguments for reform.

But this is authoritarianism by stealth.

The maximum prison sentence for breaches of the OSA is currently two years but this could increase which will have a significant chilling effect on journalists investigating government wrongdoing. More worrying still is the distinction now being made between espionage and so-called "unauthorised disclosure offences" (ie, leaks to journalists). The government believes "there are cases where an unauthorised disclosure may be as, or more, serious in terms of intent and/or damage": a large-scale digital disclosure could benefit a number of hostile actors, whereas espionage is usually carried out by a single state. The effect is that a journalist in receipt of secret documents could face a longer sentence than a spy.

Where the government really lets its authoritarian slip show, however, is in a section of the consultation about the number of successful prosecutions under existing legislation. The truth is that the record here is woeful. The government argument is as follows: "This is primarily due to the sensitive nature of the evidence that would typically be required to be disclosed in order to bring prosecutions, but also because of the age of the legislation, which means many of the offences are not designed for the modern world. Prosecutions are...rare."

This is nonsense. In most cases, prosecutions fail because they should not have been brought in the first place.

I have since been involved in two other high-profile cases, both of which

ABOVE: Katherine Gun leaving the Old Bailey in 2004, after charges against her were dropped.

collapsed. The first was of GCHQ whistleblower Katharine Gun who leaked details of a covert operation to fix the vote at the UN Security Council before the 2003 Iraq War.

The problem here was not disclosure of evidence of the crime (Gun confessed) but disclosure that would lead to ministerial embarrassment.

The second case involved a Foreign Office official, Derek Pasquill, who leaked details of government policy on radical Islam in 2006. In this case there were serious questions over whether any of his disclosures should have been covered by the OSA in the first place.

For those who care about free speech and democracy, the most serious concern should be the government's resistance to a public interest defence.

Gun and Pasquill acted in the public interest to reveal uncomfortable truths for the government. If the new legislation had been in place then, the pair may well have been sent to prison.

Boris Johnson, the UK's journalist prime minister, has said he doesn't want to see a world where people are prosecuted for doing their public duty. These proposals will do just that. ✖

Martin Bright is acting editor of Index on Censorship. A longer version of this piece appeared in the British Journalism Review

> The effect, in practice, is that a journalist in receipt of secret documents could face a longer sentence than a spy

50(03):104/104|DOI:10.1177/03064220211048881